D0127727

1

Table of Contents

Introduction - - - - - - - - - 5

Examination Overview - - - - - - - - 7

Scoring - - - - - - - - - - 9

Creating a Study Plan and Test Strategy - - - - - 11

Timing the Test - - - - - - - - - 13

Staying Calm, Cool and Collected - - - - - - 15

Critical Reading Skills: Analyzing and Interpreting Good Writing - - - 19

Types of Creative Non-Fiction - - - - - - - 23

Types of Fiction - - - - - - - - - 29

Understanding the English Language - - - - - - 31

Rhetorical Strategies and Devices - - - - - - 39

Using Rhetorical Tools in Your Writing - - - - - - 43

Rhetorical Errors and Mistakes - - - - - - - 47

What You'll Be Writing - - - - - - - - 51

Practice Test 1 - - - - - - - - - 81

Practice Test 2 - - - - - - - - - 125

Practice Test 3 - - - - - - - - - 165

Practice Test 4 - - - - - - - - - 209

Introduction

The Advanced Placement English Language and Composition class is designed to provide students with the skills necessary to read and write creative and thoughtful non-fiction, including essays of all sorts. During the course, you've had the opportunity to read and analyze older and modern creative non-fiction; many students, however, take the AP English Language and Composition Exam without having taken an AP English Language and Composition course. You can succeed on the test whether you've taken the class or not, particularly with some smart preparation in rhetoric and composition. Students who haven't taken an AP English Language and Composition course may have taken standard English courses, the AP English Literature course or other helpful classes.

The English Language and Composition Exam provides students with the opportunity to gain college credit, typically in place of an introductory composition course at a four-year college. Even colleges and universities that do not award credit for AP courses and tests may allow you to move on to a more advanced course, skipping the standard Introduction to Composition or English 101 course. It is important to realize that your score on the test determines whether or not you will receive college credit.

Preparing for the English Language and Composition exam is a process, one involving more practice than study, particularly if you're already a strong reader and writer. There are no facts or figures to memorize for this test, but you can review reading skills, grammar, and particularly rhetoric. You will be able to practice your composition skills and have the opportunity to look critically at your own work as you prepare for the test. Sample essays help you to understand AP English Language and Composition Exam grading and scoring to improve your own writing. Finally, practice tests including both multiple choice and free response questions allow you to spot your weak points, assess your skills and master the AP exam essay.

Examination Overview

Total Testing Time: Three hours and 15 minutes

Multiple Choice Questions:

- 50 to 55 Questions
- 60 minutes

The multiple choice section of the test contains five to seven reading passages, with eight to ten questions. On the English Language and Composition Exam, these passages can be fiction, non-fiction, biographies, essays, letters or speeches. Reading passages will vary in subject and style. You should expect to see both relatively modern passages, dating from the 19th century onward, and older passages, from the 18th century or earlier. Passages do not include introductory material and often will not have a title. In many cases, the reading passages are associated with only a date, rather than a full credit and citation. While passages will be examples of good-quality writing, they are unlikely to be especially entertaining. The questions will refer to the associated reading passage. We'll talk more about strategy later in this guide.

Free Response Questions

- 15 minutes reading time in total for the three essays. You may allot this time as you choose, dividing it evenly or focusing on the synthesis essay.
- 120 minutes writing time for all three essays. You may work on whichever essay you prefer first.

There are three essay questions included on the exam, each with a different focus. The test includes reading passages and free response prompts for each question. The first essay requires that you analyze a passage by providing a thorough exposition. The second essay is argumentative and should present a position in response to a statement or reading passage. Your response can be in agreement or may oppose the subject of the essay. Finally, the third essay requires that you synthesize or bring together information from different passages or sources provided. You'll find more in-depth information about each of these later in this text.

Scoring

The test is scored on a scale of 1 to 5. A score of 5 is extremely well qualified to receive college credit, while a score of one is not qualified to receive college credit. While colleges and universities use scores differently, a score of 4-5 is equivalent to an A or B. A score of 3 is approximately similar to a C, while a score of 1-2 is comparable to a D or F. The examination is scored on a curve, adjusted for difficulty each year. In this way, your test score is equivalent to the same score achieved on a different year. The curve is different each year, depending upon the test.

Scores of 4 to 5 are widely accepted by colleges and universities; however, scores of 3 or lower may provide less credit or none at all. More elite schools may require a score of 5 for credit and some schools vary the required score depending upon the department. You will need to review the AP policies at your college or university to better understand scoring requirements and credit offered. While you'll take the AP English Language and Composition Examination in May, your scores will arrive in July. You can have your scores sent to the college of your choosing, or, if you're testing after your junior year, simply wait until you're ready to apply to the colleges of your choice.

Scoring on the multiple choice section of the examination is straightforward. You receive one point for each correct answer. There are no penalties for an incorrect answer or a skipped question. If you are unsure, you should guess. Even a random guess provides you a one in four chance of a point. If you can narrow down the choices just a bit, your chances increase and, along with them, your possible test score.

Each of the three essays receives a score from 0 to 9. A high-scoring essay answers the question thoroughly and completely, shows composition skill, rhetoric, and correct grammar and language. A score of zero or a blank indicates remarkably poor writing or an essay that does not address the subject provided. These essays are typically graded by high school or college English teachers and professors. Each reader reads only one type of essay and will not see the other essays or your multiple test score. Most of the essays, around 65 percent, receive a score of between 4 and 6 for each essay. There is not an intentional curve; this is the typical scoring range.

Readers are trained using sample student essays. They are given examples of a perfect scoring essay, an average essay and a low scoring essay. You'll find similar essay examples later in this guide for your own reference. The essay readers score the essay holistically. They assign a single number score, not broken down in any way. If your essay is grammatically perfect, but poorly organized, their overall impression is likely to be poor, resulting in a poor to average score. On the other hand, a remarkably insightful essay, even if there are some grammatical or syntax errors, may receive a very high score, as the scorer is likely to be impressed with the work. During reader training, test readers are taught to grade according to these sample guidelines.

In total, approximately 25 percent of students taking the examination will receive a score of 4 or 5. More than 40 percent of students will receive a score of a 1 or 2. About 33 percent of students receive a score of 3 on the test. With the curve creating these percentages, you can expect that almost 60 percent of students score a passing grade on the examination. Smart practice and preparation can help you score in that 60 percent, rather than in the 40 percent of students who will receive no credit for their work on the AP Language and Composition exam.

Creating a Study Plan and Test Strategy

This guide is designed to provide you with the opportunity to improve your reading and writing skills, practice for the AP English Language and Composition Exam and develop a thorough understanding of what is expected for a high-scoring free response essay. With good preparation, you improve your chances of receiving a 4 or 5 and thus, have a better chance of entering college with credits under your belt.

You may use this guide in one of two ways. First, you can simply work through it in order, from chapter one through the practice tests at the end of the book. This will provide you with ample preparation for the examination, ideally over a period of several weeks or even longer. You should take this approach if you have time to prepare for the exam or will be taking the exam without taking an AP English Language and Composition class.

Students working through the entire guide should allow time each day for study and preparation. Some of that study time should be spent directly working through this guide; however, time spent critically reading material similar to that used on the examination is also helpful. Expect to allow approximately three hours per chapter for this guide, not including the introduction and study strategies chapter, for a total of around 33 hours of study time. If you've got six weeks to prepare for the test, you should schedule around five to six hours per week. You may need more or less time, depending upon your familiarity with the material.

If you have less time to prepare or have taken an AP Language and Composition course, you may wish to take one of the practice tests first. Score your test using the included answer sheet, sample essays and sample scored essays. Critically review your own work or ask a friend or teacher to help review your work and determine your weaknesses. Review those sections of this guide with special care to help improve your score on the AP Language and Composition Examination. Skip chapters that you feel confident about to reduce your prep time.

This study guide prepares you to read critically, providing you with the tools for success on the multiple choice portion of the examination. Critical reading includes reading comprehension, an understanding of rhetoric and composition, and the ability to identify both details and larger themes. It also helps you to write critically, or succeed on the free response questions. You'll work on different types of essays and writing, using rhetorical tools in your own writing, review key points of English grammar and have the opportunity to look at how the AP free response questions are scored, with examples of both high-and low-scoring essays. Finally, three full-length sample tests allow you to practice for the examination.

Timing the Test

Understanding how to time your work on the AP English Language and Composition test will help you to reduce your stress level and get the best score possible. While timing strategies vary, having one will help you avoid a serious risk: running out of time on the test and leaving questions unanswered or essays unfinished. Remember to take a watch! Even if you usually don't wear one, you'll want one for test day, and you will not be allowed to look at your smartphone.

The multiple-choice section of the exam consists of 50 to 55 questions over a 60-minute test period. While this works out to a relatively easy rate of one minute per question, you also need time to read and analyze the passages. The simplest way to time this portion of the test is to allot your time in blocks. The test consists of five to seven passages, so you have between 8 ½ and 12 minutes per passage in which to read, take any notes you need, and answer all of the associated questions. You'll need to do the mental math to track your own time when you open your examination book on the day of the test.

If, on test day, you discover your examination has six passages, with 8 to 9 questions each, you have ten minutes per passage. Plan to allow no more than four minutes to read the passage. Make notes as you read, making certain to catch the main idea of the passage, topic sentences for each paragraph, and any key details, as well as the author's point of view. These minimal notes, even just a word or two or an underline, can help you to answer questions quickly and accurately.

Begin answering the questions. Answer those you know with certainty or relative certainty at once on the first pass. Quickly review the lines noted in the question for detail questions. Make a second pass, using the process of elimination to reduce the possible answers, ideally, from five to two. Of those two or three answers, make your best guess and move on to the next question. You may want to mark these answers in your test book with a check or another mark. If you have extra time after completing all of the questions, don't hesitate to return to these questions, review your answers and take additional time to reread portions of the passage and correct these questions, if needed.

You have 120 minutes of time for the three free response questions, plus an additional 15-minute reading period. This is not included in the 40 minutes of writing time allowed for each essay. Plan to allot your 40 minutes of time carefully. Take the first three to five minutes to create an outline for your essay. Plan to use the final three to five minutes to review your work. This leaves you with 30 to 34 minutes of total writing time, assuming you've already completed the reading. Some students find it helpful to use the majority of their reading time for the hardest of the three essays, the synthesis essay. While the preparation and review time results in less time to write, your outline will keep you on-track and the review time will allow you time for corrections or to improve your essay's conclusion.

Staying Calm, Cool and Collected

Conquering test anxiety can help you to succeed on AP exams. Test anxiety is common and, if it's mild, can help keep you alert and on-task. Unfortunately, if you suffer from serious shakes, it may leave you struggling to focus, cause you to make careless errors, and create potential panic.

- Allow plenty of time for test preparation. Work slowly and methodically. Cramming doesn't help and will leave you depleted and exhausted.
- Remember to stay healthy. Sleep enough, eat right, and get regular exercise.
- Practice breathing exercises to use on test day to help with anxiety. Deep breathing is one of the easiest, fastest and most effective ways to reduce physical symptoms of anxiety.

While these strategies won't eliminate test anxiety, they can help you to reach exam day at your mental best, prepared to succeed.

The night before the test, just put away the books. More preparation isn't going to make a difference. Read something light, watch a favorite show, go for a relaxing walk and go to bed. Get up early enough in the morning to have a healthy breakfast. If you normally drink coffee, don't skip it, but if you don't regularly consume caffeine, avoid it. It'll just make you jittery. Allow time to reach the testing location and get your desk set up and ready before the examination starts.

What to Take

- A sweatshirt or sweater, in case the testing room is cold.
- A bottle of water.
- At least two No. 2 pencils, sharpened.
- At least two black or blue ink pens.
- A wristwatch

A quick note here: there's no need to take paper along. You'll receive not only the test booklet, but also additional scratch paper to take notes and make outlines for your free response questions.

Tackling the Test

Some people don't find testing terribly anxiety-inducing. If that's you, feel free to skip this section. These tips and techniques are designed specifically for students who do struggle with serious test anxiety.

- Control your breathing. Taking short, fast breaths increases physical anxiety. Maintain a normal to slow breathing pattern.
- Remember your test timing strategies. Timing strategies can help provide you with confidence that you're staying on track.
- Focus on one question at a time. While you may become overwhelmed thinking about the entire test, a single question or a single passage often seems more manageable.
Get up and take a break. While this should be avoided if at all possible, if you're feeling so anxious that you're concerned you will be sick, are dizzy or are feeling unwell, take a bathroom break or sharpen your pencil. Use this time to practice breathing exercises. Return to the test as soon as you're able.

Using the Sample Tests

This guide includes three full-length sample AP English Language and Composition tests. While these tests familiarize you with the format and type of passages and questions you will see on the test, they can also help you practice for test day, learn to employ your timing and test strategies and reduce your anxiety on test day.

Take the practice tests in a quiet, comfortable environment. Mimic the test environment as much as possible. Time the sections of the test correctly and avoid getting up and down, fetching a drink, or having a snack. Plan to take the entire practice test in a single setting, just as you would on test day. Even if you can't do this for each of the practice tests, make time to do it for at least one of them, so you've had the full test experience once before the big day.

If you find after taking one round of multiple-choice questions that you're pleased with your score, you can focus your test practice on the free response questions. You'll find a total of 12 free response questions included with these practice tests, but you'll find many more on the AP web site if you'd like additional practice for the free response questions. If this is case, be aware that the synthesis essay is a relatively new addition to the test.

Critical Reading Skills: Analyzing and Interpreting Good Writing

There are a number of aspects to smart and skillful critical reading. Understanding all of them will help you to recognize the author's main idea, point of view and key details. These aspects of your reading are critical to success on the multiple choice portion of the AP English Language and Composition examination.

1. Finding the Main Idea
2. Identifying the Author
3. Reading for Tone
4. Recognizing the Author's Point of View
5. Finding Key Details

You were probably taught how to identify the main idea of a piece around the time you learned to read. In kindergarten and first grade, your teacher asked what the story was about, what the paragraph was about, or what you'd learned in the lesson. These are the very same skills you need to use to find the main idea on the AP English Language and Composition exam. Unfortunately, the passages are significantly more complex and finding the main idea may not be so easy.

In most cases, the passages on the AP Language exam do not include a title, caption, author or context. You'll be faced with several paragraphs of text, with no idea whether it is fiction or non-fiction, where it was published or who wrote it. You will, in most cases, have a date associated with the passage, but nothing more. Since these passages are excerpts, you may or may not have a complete work or a complete portion of a work. You cannot rely upon introductory paragraphs to provide the main idea of the passage.

To find the main idea, read through the entire passage, from start to finish. If there is an introductory paragraph to the passage, as there may be if it is a complete essay or the beginning of a chapter, pay special attention to this paragraph. Consider the final paragraph in the same way; however, these tricks may not always apply. If you don't have a clear introduction or conclusion, you can still find the main idea of the passage. Ask yourself what the author hopes to convey in this passage. Simplify that to a single sentence. There may be a topic sentence in the passage. If so, underline or highlight the sentence. If not, jot down the answer to your question. This is the main idea of the passage and is essential to your understanding and interpretation of the reading.

Most of the time when you read, you know who the author is. That's typically not the case on the AP English Language and Composition exam. You may be given somewhat more information on the free response passages than for the multiple choice questions. While you may not know the author's name, you can still, to some extent, answer the question of "who." As you read, think about the likely author. You will likely know when the passage was written, so imagine who wrote it. Was it a man or a woman? A scholar, a professional writer, an everyday citizen? You don't need a name, but a mental image can help you answer other key big-picture questions essential to understanding passages on the test, particularly for the free response questions. If you do know the author's name, think about what you know. For instance, if you are reading a portion of a speech by Susan B. Anthony, you might know that she was a suffragette active in the late 19th century. This provides you with some immediate context and information helpful to your essay response.

While the main idea of the passage is important, you also need to understand the author's tone, point-of-view and intent. These components are especially important in non-fiction works, as they may help you to understand why the author wrote what they wrote, develop a mental context for the piece and correctly categorize and analyze the passage. These three components are similar and are closely related to one another.

The tone of writing is very much like tone of voice. A piece of writing can be warm and friendly, cold and scholarly, humorous or angry. Consider for instance, the tone of a child's book, like Winnie the Pooh. It's friendly and affectionate. On the other hand, a political editorial, even one in your local paper, may be angry and frustrated. While tone is sometimes straightforward, it isn't always. In some cases, tone can help you to recognize irony, sarcasm or other rhetorical devices. A simple sentence, like "The dress was lovely" can mean two very different things. In a piece with a neutral or positive tone, it likely means that the speaker really did believe the dress was attractive. In a piece with a more negative tone, the speaker may have thought the dress quite ugly.

The author's point-of-view, intent or perspective may color their writing, even in relatively neutral pieces. In fiction, an author may favor one character over another. If the main idea answers "what," point-of-view or perspective answers "why". Why did the author write this passage or piece? Why were specific words used? The answers may vary. Perhaps the author wanted to persuade the reader of something, inform the reader about a subject or share information about a character in a fictional story. The author may have simply written with the goal of entertaining the reader.

In some cases, the author may be very open about his or her point-of-view. It may be stated, in an introductory paragraph or elsewhere, or obvious, particularly in an argumentative or persuasive essay. In an informational or entertaining piece, it may be more difficult to recognize the author's perspective or point-of-view. The point-of-view in a work of fiction is often especially ambiguous. You may, in some instances, only be able to identify point-of-view from a narrative perspective, like first person. What you learned about tone and intent may help you to determine the author's perspective, as can your answers to "why" the author wrote this piece.

While the big picture is especially important for the free response questions, to succeed on the multiple choice questions, you'll need not only the big picture, but also the small details. As you read, make note of names, dates and locations. For a piece of non-fiction, dates and locations may be very specific or less so; however, they are rarely so specific for works of fiction. In fictional works, think in broad terms of the setting, for instance, a wealthy home in 19th century England or Berlin sometime during World War II. The details will often answer questions of "when" and "where," but will also bring their own answers to "who" and "what".

- What is the main idea?
- Who wrote the piece?
- Why was it written?
- When are the important dates?
- Where the piece is set?

You can expect to see aspects of all of these elements in the multiple choice questions on the exam.

Types of Creative Non-Fiction

The types of essays are frequently broken down into several basic forms or modes of discourse. Sometimes abbreviated as EDNA, one classification identifies four types of creative non-fiction as Exposition, Narration, Description and Argumentation. It should be noted that these categories are not exclusive, and you may encounter works of non-fiction or essays that do not fit into the EDNA scheme. A similar system breaks works of non-fiction down into four types, including the expository, persuasive, analytical and argumentative. As you can see, there are some overlaps between these two schemes, including the expository and argumentative essays.

For the purposes of the AP Language and Composition examination, you should thoroughly understand all types of creative non-fiction; however, it is smart to focus on the expository, persuasive, analytical and argumentative essay types. You're most likely to see examples of these essays on the examination. You will also need to write an expository essay, an argumentative essay and one essay that synthesizes information from multiple sources, incorporating a variety of writing strategies.

The essay is a relatively short piece of writing; however, there are a number of types of longer works of non-fiction, some of which fit into these categories. Longer forms of non-fiction include biographies, autobiographies, and memoirs, letters and journals, history, science, political treatises and more. Articles in the media are also non-fiction, but are not typically considered essays. Books on history and biographies are often narrative, while a book about science may be analytical or expository. Some pieces, both short and long, are less easy to categorize. These may include more personal writings of various sorts, sharing the author's inner thoughts and feelings.

The expository essay explains something. It may be an idea, a theme, an issue or even simply a single sentence. The expository essay may discuss a personal response to an event, work of art or literature, debate or discussion. Of these four essay types, the expository essay often most closely fits the essay format students learned in grade school or middle school. The essay begins with an introduction, including a strong topic sentence or thesis. Body paragraphs in the essay provide evidence to back up the thesis statement or topic sentence. A concluding paragraph or paragraphs restate the thesis or main idea of the essay.

The persuasive essay attempts to convince the reader of something, whether it be social, political or more personal. The persuasive essay requires a strong point-of-view, along with evidence to back up that opinion. The evidence should be factual, rather than emotional, and the essay should appeal specifically to the intended reader. For instance, a persuasive essay about improving school lunches aimed at parents might emphasize the immediate health benefits for the children, while one intended for a larger audience could focus on the larger benefits of lower health care costs and reduced obesity rates. Both arguments rely upon facts; however, each is designed to appeal to a specific audience. A successful persuasive essay convinces the reader that your view is correct, or opens the reader's mind to the possibility that you might be correct.

While a persuasive essay attempts to convince the reader of the author's point-of-view, the analytic essay breaks down and analyzes a topic. It investigates the topic in a systematic and thoughtful way. A well-written analytical essay does not restate the topic, but tackles it piece by piece. An analytical essay may focus on a specific reading, a poem, a work of art or another topic. Each part of the topic should be considered in relation to the other parts and to the whole. The persuasive essay needs a thesis paragraph, rather than a thesis sentence. The point-of-view should be clear; however, the thesis paragraph should also set forth the basis for the analysis. These directional sentences will guide the remainder of the essay. Analytic essays should directly refer to the work in question, paraphrasing or quoting where appropriate to reinforce the author's arguments. The body paragraphs should relate to the directional sentences in the thesis paragraph. Unlike some essays, an analytic essay should integrate the author's personal responses. Like other types of essays, the analytic essay ends with a conclusion, in this case, one that stresses the accuracy of the argument and analysis.

An argumentative essay is similar to a persuasive essay; however, an argumentative essay specifically opposes another point-of-view. In many cases, the argumentative essay requires a relatively substantial amount of research to craft a thorough and well-constructed argument in defense of the author's perspective. While a persuasive essay attempts to convince the reader of the author's opinion, an argumentative essay shows that your point-of-view is more correct or accurate than another perspective. Argumentative essays must begin with a clear statement, rather than a question or vague idea. Evidence should support the author's argument. The evidence should include not only points supporting the author's argument, but also document the flaws in the contrasting argument. The conclusion should clearly restate and support the author's position.

The narrative essay tells a story. In most cases, the information is presented in chronological order. While a narrative essay or piece of non-fiction writing may resemble fiction in some cases, the people, events, and other facts in the writing are true, having all happened. They are not invented or imagined. In many cases, however, the narrative essay includes most of the elements common to a fictional story. There are characters, a setting, a plot, a climax and a conclusion. Other forms of narratives, like book reports or summaries, may not include these elements.

During your English Language and Composition course, as well as other high school classes, you've likely written some of these essay types. In most cases, you started with the simple five-paragraph essay form, consisting of an introduction with a thesis statement or topic sentence, three body paragraphs and a conclusion. Hopefully, you've had the opportunity to expand those skills, build upon them and practice all of these types of creative non-fiction writing. If not, you'll have the chance to master them as you prepare for the AP Language and Composition examination. Keep these essay types in mind as you prepare for and take the test:

- Expository: Explain it.
- Persuasive: Convince the reader.
- Analytical: Break it down.
- Argumentative: Win them over.
- Narrative: Tell a story.
-

The following definitions are drawn from W.F. Webster's 1902 *English Composition and Literature:*

1. *Narration is that form of discourse which recounts events in a sequence.* It includes stories, novels, romances, biographies, some books of travel, and some histories.
2. *Description is that form of discourse which aims to present a picture.* It seldom occurs alone, but it is usually found in combination with the other forms of discourse.
3. *Exposition is that form of discourse which seeks to explain a term or a proposition.* Text-books, books of information, theses, most histories, many magazine articles, and newspaper leaders are of this class of literature.
4. *Argument is that form of discourse which has for its object the proof of the truth or falsity of a proposition.*
5. *Persuasion is that form of discourse the purpose of which is to influence the will.*

These definitions can help to clarify the types of non-fiction essays you will need to read and write for the AP examination. You may find, in many cases, that a single essay includes elements of multiple types of creative non-fiction. For instance, an expository essay may recount a short narrative episode or an analytic essay may include elements of description. This list is not complete, but does provide you with a basic understanding essential for the test.

Types of Fiction

Fiction is typically divided into commercial and literary fiction. Commercial fiction includes typical trade paperbacks, usually belonging to a genre like romance or horror. You won't find examples of commercial fiction on the AP Language and Composition exam. While most of the work included on the exam is likely to be non-fiction, rather than literature, you may see examples of literary fiction. Literary fiction is identified not by genre, but by quality. It exhibits excellent writing, original thought and style. While the AP Language and Composition course focuses on functional language and rhetoric, it is possible that you will see examples of literary fiction. You should; however, keep in mind that the analysis of these pieces is not, in a Language and Composition course or test, literary. It is, like the analysis of non-fiction, rhetorical.

Common types of fiction writing include the short story, the novella and the novel. These all contain the same basic elements and are separated by length. If you do encounter literature on the AP Language examination, you are likely to see only a passage from one of these, rather than an entire piece. Other types of literature may also appear on the test, particularly in the free response question. This includes poetry of various sorts.

The addition of fiction to the test may provide a challenge for some students, particularly those who sought out the AP Language and Composition course to avoid literary studies. As a student, you should remember that the works of literature included on the test are not intended for literary analysis. Your analysis of these works does not, fundamentally, differ from any study of non-fiction. You should consider the subject, content, and the use of rhetorical devices in the text.

Understanding the English Language

Comprehending formal aspects of writing is only one part of the AP Language and Composition exam. You also need a thorough understanding of grammar, parts of speech and sentence structure. You won't be specifically tested on these, and minor errors are often overlooked in a good essay. However, understanding and composing sentences requires a thorough understanding of the English language. Somewhat more ambiguously, you also need to write with a degree of stylistic sophistication. Stylistic sophistication means that your writing is mature and well-crafted, with a complex and varied range of sentences.

The purpose of this guide is not to teach grammar; however, in the reference section you'll find a number of links to sites specializing in grammar, recommended by the AP Board, including spelling, parts of speech and common grammar problems. If you're a strong reader and writer, you can likely skip over this section entirely. You may want to assess samples of your own writing to spot and correct any grammatical weaknesses you may find. Talk to your AP Language and Composition instructor or your English teacher if you're not sure if you have any problem areas. They may have recognized weaknesses or challenges in your writing and may be able to guide you in your studies and preparation for the test. You won't be asked specific questions on grammar on the test, and can make some grammatical errors without risking a poor score on the free response questions.

Just as you may want to brush up on your grammar, you should also work to expand your vocabulary. While there are not specific, published lists of vocabulary words for the AP English Language and Composition exam, tools and lists intended for ACT or SAT preparation are an effective option. There are a number of ways to improve your vocabulary:

- Traditional options include making flashcards, with the word on one side and the definition on the other.
- You can do the same using an online flashcard site if you prefer.
- Many students find it quick and effective to work on vocabulary with a smartphone app or something similar. These teach you unfamiliar words, allowing you to work on your vocabulary whenever time allows, for instance, while waiting on an appointment or sitting at lunch.
- Spend time reading relatively complex material and maintaining a word list.

When you find an unknown word, add it to your list along with the definition. While repetition is an effective way to add terms to your vocabulary, depending upon your strengths, you may find memory tools, like mnemonics or linking the word to an image, to be helpful. A good vocabulary isn't just helpful for the free response questions. You may also find vocabulary questions on the multiple choice portion of the AP Language and Composition Examination.

While repetitive study is helpful for vocabulary review and enhancement, understanding common root words, prefixes and suffixes can also help you to decode new and unfamiliar words you may encounter on the AP Language and Composition exam. The following lists of prefixes and suffixes include some common ones found in high-quality writing, like the examples you will see on the AP test. Understanding root words, prefixes and suffixes can help you to understand unfamiliar words and improve your chances of a correct answer.

Prefixes

a-, an-: without	di-, dis-: apart	mis-: badly	pre-: before
ab-: away from	epi-: upon	mono-: one	pro-: forward, supporting
ad-, at-: to, toward	equ-: equal	non-: the reverse of	re-: again
anti-: against	ex-, e-: away	ob-: in front	se-: apart
bi-: two	in-, im-: into	omni-: everywhere	sub-: under
cir-: around	in-, ig-, ir-: not	per-: through	trans-: across
co-, com-, con-: together	inter-: between	poly-: many	un-: one
de-: away from, down	mal-: bad	post-: after	un-: not

Suffixes

-ble: able to	-ion: the act of	-ness: quality of
-acious, -al: like	-ism: the practice of or support of	-ory: a place or thing for
-ancy, -ance: the act of	-ist: one who does	-ous, -ose: full of
-ant, -er, -or: one who	-ity, -ty-, -y: practice of	-ship: the skill of or ability to
-ar, -ary: connected with	-ive: with the nature of	-some: full of
-ence: quality of	-less: lacking	-tude: the state of or ability to
-ful: full of	-logy: study of	-y: somewhat
-ic, -il, -ile: of, like	-ment: state of, act of	

The possible root words for the English language include examples in Latin, Greek and other languages. You'll find links to tables containing root word lists in the "For Further Study" section at the end of this guide. While it's unlikely you'll master all of the possible root words, understanding some of the most common will help you with challenging reading and multiple choice questions on the test.

While review of vocabulary will help you on the free response questions, you also need to make sure you can understand and assess vocabulary in context for the multiple choice portion of the examination. Many words have more than one meaning or can vary in meaning depending upon other words in the sentence. When asked to choose a definition for a word on the AP English Language exam, be sure you reread the sentence or sentences referenced in the question. You should also read at least the sentence before and the one after for the best understanding of context. Choose the best option from those available to fit into the sentence or passage, rather than the one that might be the most common meaning of the word.

When you encounter a familiar word and you understand how it is used in the context of the passage or sentence, these multiple-choice questions will go quickly. If you are not familiar with the word, you can employ a smart vocabulary strategy to increase your chances of a correct answer. You may have, in school, been taught the PAVE strategy, or "Predict, Associate, Verify, Evaluate". Essentially, this process requires that you predict the definition of a word, associate it with a mental image, verify the definition and evaluate your prediction. Obviously, you won't have access to a dictionary to verify definitions during the AP exam. You can, however, predict an answer, associate it with a mental image and evaluate your prediction.

For instance, if a question asks the meaning of the word "impeccable" in the following short passage, "He was meticulous in his dress. His shirt was always pressed, his trousers creased and his shoes shined. He looked impeccable." In this case, you don't need to fill in another word. You do need to know that the correct definition for impeccable, in this case, would be faultless. You might predict that the answer is "perfect" or something similar. You can form a mental image of a perfectly dressed man. When you review the answers available, you can evaluate your prediction. If your choices are faultless, slovenly, average, and dreadful, only one of these words fits your prediction of "perfect". The same scheme you might have used in grade school applies, even on a test you're taking for potential college credit.

Stylistic sophistication has everything to do with your syntax, style, tone and point-of-view. We discussed interpreting tone and point-of-view as a reader, but working with these elements as a writer is somewhat different.

- Syntax: The ordering of words in a sentence.
- Style: The manner of expression
- Tone: Attitude, mood or sentiment revealed by the style
- Point-of-view: Stance revealed by style and tone

In your reading and writing, you can create a simple equation. The combination of style and tone equals point-of-view. Broadly all of these elements combine to create the complete image of the writer's overall attitude or purpose. As a writer, these elements together provide your work with the quality and stylistic maturity expected for a high-scoring essay on the AP Language and Composition examination.

Style doesn't mean your writing has to be flowery, wordy or overly pretentious; in fact, it shouldn't be. Your essays should be clear, logical and concise, but they should read well and be engaging and interesting to your reader. Look at the difference between these two short paragraphs.

> It was rainy that day. I was tired. I went to class. I went home. It was cold in the house. I did homework. I went to bed.

> I was tired on that cold, rainy day. I struggled through class and trudged home, to be greeted by a chilly house. After homework, I fell into bed, exhausted.

These two sample paragraphs mean exactly the same thing. Both present a short narrative about someone's day. In the first example, the sentences create a short, staccato rhythm. It's unappealing to read, the language is dull, and the sentence structure is simplistic. The second shows varied sentence structure and vocabulary. It offers words that are more descriptive, creating the image of a cold, dreary and miserable day. Even when the content is the same, the use of syntax and word choice dramatically changes writing.

Your style also sheds light on your overall point-of-view and the impression created by your writing. Imagine two argumentative essays, both discussing the death penalty. Later, in our discussion of logos, pathos and ethos in the chapter on rhetoric, you will learn about the impressions that your words make. Think about your impressions of each of the following short paragraphs. Again, the overall message of the content is similar.

> The death penalty is horrible! Innocent people are executed for crimes they did not commit. Death penalty advocates say that it reduces crime, but that is not true.

> The death penalty may offer closure to some families of victims of violent crime, but this punishment comes at a high cost. During the appeals process, several defendants on death row have been cleared by DNA evidence, shedding some doubt on the "guilty beyond a reasonable doubt" argument. Fortunately, these individuals were, at the least, able to walk free, having lost years, but not their lives. While we might hope the threat of the death penalty could serve as a deterrent to violent crimes, crime rates are highest in regions that make use of the death penalty.

The first paragraph shows the same sort of weak syntax and word choice seen in the examples above; however, in this case, it also fails to employ any rhetorical strategies or devices. In the second example, we can see the use of logos, ethos, and pathos (more on this later.) The passage offers up information from reputable sources, appeals to the emotions, and is well-reasoned, offering up valid arguments against the possible benefits of the death penalty.

Further in this text, you will find examples of high, middle and low scoring Advanced Placement Language and Composition essays, helping you to visualize and understand these rhetorical concepts and key writing skills in more detail.

Rhetorical Strategies and Devices

The Merriam-Webster dictionary defines rhetoric as "the art or skill of speaking or writing formally and effectively, especially as a way to persuade or influence people." The focus of the reading and writing components of the AP Language and Composition course is an understanding of this art or skill of writing formally and effectively. While we've already reviewed various types of writing, you also need to understand the rhetorical strategies or writing techniques and devices or specific tools used in skillful writing of all types. Rhetoric is a relatively broad heading and includes essential elements key to persuading or convincing your reader, parts of writing and speech, and even fallacies you should avoid.

There are three elements to classical rhetoric, drawn from the ancient Greek philosopher Aristotle; logos, ethos and pathos. These three elements combine to form successful writing, particularly persuasive writing. Logos appeals to reason and logic, relying upon objective facts and statistics. Ethos relies upon the credibility of the author or the author's sources. For a student, ethos would include careful citation of good-quality source material. Pathos appeals to emotions and desires, rather than logic. You may notice that these three words; logos, pathos and ethos have parallels in English, like logic, pathological and ethical.

Imagine employing these rhetorical strategies in an argumentative essay about drunk driving laws. An essay relying on pathos might use the sad, personal stories of those killed to argue for stronger laws against drunk driving. The same topic, in a very logical way, might cite numbers killed by drunk drivers and drunk driving statistics. To appeal to ethos, you might use reliable sources, like the National Department of Transportation. All three elements can produce a good essay, used alone or together.

Recognizing these rhetorical devices helps you to understand good writing and allows you to improve your own writing. The following list of rhetorical strategies is not complete and you may think of others you would like to add to this list. As you review the list of rhetorical devices, think of examples you might be familiar with in your own reading.

During the weeks prior to the examination, look for these rhetorical devices in your readings. You can find definitions for these online; however, some of these are likely familiar, including alliteration, epithet, and oxymoron. The table below provides a relatively thorough list of possible rhetorical devices.

Alliteration	Antithesis	Climax	Epizeuxis	Metanoia	Polysyndeton
Allusion	Apophasis	Conduplicatio	Eponym	Metaphor	Procatalepsis
Amplification	Aporia	Diacope	Exemplum	Metonymy	Rhetorical Question
Anacoluthon	Aposiopesis	Dirimens Copulatio	Sentential Adverb	Onomatopoeia	Scesis Onomaton
Anadiplosis	Apostrophe	Distinctio	Hyperbaton	Oxymoron	Sententia
Analogy	Appositive	Enthymeme	Hyperbole	Parallelism	Simile
Anaphora	Assonance	Enumeratio	Hypophora	Parataxis	Symploce
Antanagoge	Asyndeton	Epanalepsis	Hypotaxis	Parenthesis	Synecdoche
Antimetabole	Catachresis	Epistrophe	Litotes	Personification	Understatement
Antiphrasis	Chiasmus	Epithet	Metabasis	Pleonasm	Zeugma

Rhetorical devices are only one part of working with words in formal speech and writing. Figurative language is also an essential part of both non-fiction and fictional writing. Figurative language can appear in a variety of forms. You can use figurative language in your writing for the AP Language exam; however, it's not essential. Examples of figurative language include:

- Aphorism: A short statement of opinion or truth
- Bombast: Pompous language
- Circumlocution: Talking around a subject or around a word
- Connotation: Suggested meanings or those that are not literal
- Denotation: A word's literal meaning
- Euphemism: Word used to avoid an unpleasant or offensive word
- Extended Metaphor: A comparison that lasts longer than a single phrase or sentence.
- Hyperbole: Exaggeration
- Imagery: Language used to convey sensory perception, sometimes treated as a synonym of figurative language.
- Irony: Stating the opposite of what is meant or a situation that is the opposite of what was expected
- Metaphor: Comparison of two unlike objects without "like" or "as"
- Oxymoron: Contradiction of two words or terms
- Paradox: Apparent contradiction of two different ideas
- Satire: Language distorted or used for comic effect
- Simile: Comparison of two unlike objects, typically using "like" or "as"
- Symbol: A word representing something it is not

Regardless of whether you opt to use figurative language in your writing, you should be able to identify it for the multiple choice questions on the examination. You might, for instance, be asked which type of figurative language was represented by a line of text. If you don't know the difference between a simile and a metaphor, you are likely to answer incorrectly. Recognizing rhetorical devices and figurative language on a basic level will improve your writing, but is essential to show your comprehension of the reading skills learned in English Language and Composition.

Using Rhetorical Tools in Your Writing

While you will need to understand and recognize the use of rhetoric to answer multiple-choice questions on the AP Language and Composition examination, you need to incorporate these rhetorical tools into your own writing. You won't need to name or state these rhetorical strategies, and often you'll use them naturally to produce good-quality writing. Keep these basics of rhetoric in mind as you write. If you haven't taken the English Language and Composition course, you may feel overwhelmed about the rhetorical aspects of writing, but, in practical application, these are the basics of good writing, or producing a high-quality essay, that you've learned through years of English classes.

The first three of these are relatively simple and quite self-explanatory. You can use these not only when you're writing, but also when you're organizing your thoughts to begin writing your essays. Think of these as a writing strategy or plan. These three basic tools are classify, compare and contrast, and illustrate. You'll use them in different ways depending upon what you're writing.

- *Classify:* Classification is a system of breaking down information into categories. In terms of writing a good essay, classification can help you organize your thoughts, stay on topic, and maintain well-structured paragraphs. Depending upon the essay topic, your categories may be factual, related to your own thoughts or analysis, or a combination of the two. You can separate individual points or facts into your categories during the outline process or refer to these classifications as you write to stay on-topic.

- *Compare and Contrast:* Comparing and contrasting two or more items, be they essays, works of art, literature, or ideas, allows you to note the similarities and differences between these things. Similarities and differences can relate to content, style, theme, use of rhetorical devices, or other factors in a work. In order to effectively compare two things, there must be some similarities. You can also use comparisons outside the text, to help illustrate a point. This type of comparison is called an analogy. The process of comparing and contrasting requires that you select the points for comparison or contrasting. You'll classify or categorize each of these points to organize your writing.
  - While you will categorize your information, you should not discuss the two compared items separately. For instance, each paragraph should include information about one aspect of each thing, whether it is similar or different. A well-written comparison does not present all of the information about one

thing in a paragraph and another thing in the next. Integrate your similarities and differences into your writing. Combine common elements where possible. You might put all content related similarities and differences into a single paragraph and all stylistic comparisons into one paragraph.

- o For single subject essays, analogies can help the reader to understand something that may be uncommon or unknown, or to put an abstract subject in concrete terms. As an example, you might consider an explanation of depression. While your reader might understand depression as sadness, you could put this into concrete terms by explaining it as a hole you can't get out of, slipping down further every time you attempt to climb up and out of the darkness. Analogies should be used in expository essays, rather than argumentative ones. They are a tool to further your reader's understanding of the subject.
- Illustrate: For many types of essays, illustrating or giving examples in support of your main idea or thesis is essential to good writing.
  - o Choose examples that support your thesis. Avoid those that are irrelevant, unrelated, or in conflict with your facts and essay.
  - o Use transitions, like "for instance" and "for example" to introduce examples in support of your point.

Mastering these basics is essential, but understanding more complex rhetorical writing skills will help you to write a high-scoring AP essay. You may use some of these in your free response answers, but should also be able to recognize them for the multiple choice sections on the test.

- *Process Analysis:* Process analysis is a formal description for what many of us might describe as a how-to or step-by-step process. Lab reports and instructions are both examples of process analysis. Chronological narratives, even those with examples or other information included, are also considered to be a type of process analysis. Process analysis organizes something with words like first, next, and finally. It's critical to remember all of the steps in a process. Skipping one, whether in a narrative or a how-to, can confuse your reader. Fundamentally, process analysis describes how to do something or how something happened.
- *Cause and Effect:* Cause and effect provides an explanation for why something has happened. This rhetorical tool can deal with both immediate and underlying causes. For instance, if the effect is that the family was unable to pay their utility bill, the immediate cause might be that the primary wage earner was out of work. An underlying cause could be an overall economic downturn in the region. If you do opt to use cause and effect, the relationship between the two should

be clear and illustrated with examples. Include all information necessary for the reader to understand the relationship between cause and effect in this situation.

- *Definition:* In a rhetorical sense, the word definition implies more than just a short, dictionary-style definition. A rhetorical definition is typically a paragraph, providing information and explaining a term, event or activity. It might include both examples and analogies. A definition is especially important when the event, activity or term is likely to be unfamiliar to your reader.

- *Description:* Description is common in all types of essays and can be either objective or subjective, depending upon the writer's needs and intentions. In many cases, descriptions serve to keep the reader's interest, providing details about a place, experience or scene that they would not, otherwise, know. Unlike many other rhetorical strategies used in non-fiction, description does not require objectivity or even, in some cases, significant organization. You may be sharing your own understanding, perceptions, and thoughts in your description. Use concrete nouns, consider spatial relationships, and include rhetorical devices, like similes and metaphors, in your descriptions.

- *Narration:* In the simplest sense, narration is storytelling, typically in chronological order. Narratives may be told in the first person, as you're telling your own story, or in their third, if you're telling someone else's story. Narratives should move from beginning to middle to end. Include action verbs and descriptive language to bring the story to life for the reader.

- *Induction and Deduction:* Induction is a process of reaching a conclusion from the evidence presented by a number of related examples. Deduction is the process of using generalizations to draw a conclusion. In this, these two processes are the opposite of one other. Induction moves from the specific to the general and deduction from the general to the specific.

Rhetorical Errors and Mistakes

Just as the proper use of rhetoric improves writing, the improper use of some rhetorical devices weakens it. You should avoid using these in your own writing, and you need to be able to recognize them in the work of others. You may, in some instances, find examples of these sorts of rhetorical devices in the reading passages, free response passages, or as false answers in the multiple choice questions.

The argument from false authority attempts to use ethos to justify an argument; however, the source used is, in itself, inaccurate. For instance, were you to reference facts and figures about the Holocaust from a source known for Holocaust denial, this would be an example of an argument from false authority, or a false. On the same note, "You can catch a cold from wearing wet socks" would be a false argument, even if your grandmother says you can. Your sources should be logical, reliable and authoritative. For instance, legal briefs or court records would be a valid, authoritative source for a discussion of the law. A classmate, a tabloid, or something someone said on Facebook are not.

An ad hominem argument questions a point or argument on the basis of a personal fact about someone, rather than the facts. The ad hominem argument is recognizable by a shift in perspective and topic. The argument might be in some ways accurate, but the rhetoric is not. You might, for instance, read the following, "His testimony has to be incorrect, he used to use drugs." While drug use might cause questionable testimony in some circumstances, there's no clear relationship between the two. In a similar way, a red herring attempts to draw attention away from a valid argument by introducing irrelevant information, typically an entirely different issue.

The appeal to ignorance relies upon a single statement, questioning whether or not something can be proven true or false. Taking a popular topic from modern television, "No one can prove Bigfoot doesn't exist, therefore Bigfoot is real," or the reverse of this, "No one can prove Bigfoot exists, therefore Bigfoot is not real."

Theoretically, either argument could be correct, but the basis for the argument is false in both instances.

Assuming the conclusion of an argument, sometimes called begging the question, is a circular argument. It begins from an assumption that the conclusion is correct. For instance, "The visions of Nostradamus are true prophecy. Nostradamus says so." Clearly, Nostradamus cannot speak to the validity of his own visions in any way. The argument is not based upon facts or evidence in any way. A dogmatic argument is similar. This argument begins from a basic belief that the speaker is correct and cannot, in any way, be in error. Without any possibility of error, there is no potential for a valid argument.

A false cause argument or non sequitur connects unrelated facts or details. For instance, the dinosaurs became extinct because mammals were beginning to evolve. Yes, dinosaurs did become extinct around the same time small mammals were evolving; however, these two events are not related to one another, or have no causal relationship. The false cause argument may be called faulty or false causality. Faulty or false analogies are similar. These suggest that two unrelated things are related in a logical way.

A false dichotomy assumes that an argument has only two possible answers, with nothing in between. For instance, "you should eat salads every day or you won't be healthy, so eat your salad to be healthy." Obviously, there are many other healthy foods you could eat regularly to meet the same nutritional criteria. There's nothing about eating salad that guarantees health. Eating salad is not the only way to be healthy, nor does it guarantee health. This is a black and white argument, with no room for shades of gray.

A straw man argument simplifies your opponent's argument. It eliminates any possibility that the opponent could be correct or accurate by disregarding their arguments and evidence completely. In this, it frequently employs a personal attack, questioning the character of the opposition. For instance, "People who want to legalize marijuana just want to get high." In this case, suggesting that everyone who supports legalization of marijuana wants to get high or is a drug user frames their arguments as incorrect.

While pathos, or an appeal to emotion, may in some instances be a valid rhetorical tool, arguments based solely on sentiment or emotions are not. The conclusion may be correct, but the argument is not. An example of an appeal to emotion or sentiment is, "You should eat your vegetables because children are starving." Children will starve whether or not you eat your vegetables. The comment is intended to upset you, nothing more. A scare tactic is similar, but typically more exaggerated. Gun control opponents might, for instance, compare additional background check requirements to Nazi gun control regulations. Logically, the introduction of additional background checks is unrelated to Nazism; however, the idea of Nazism is frightening.

Equivocation or lying by omission tells only part of the story. This argument intentionally avoids presenting potentially contradictory or conflicting information. For instance, if asked if you'd had a beer at the party, you might answer no. Your answer is technically honest, but avoids mentioning that you had a mixed drink. The implication of the answer is that no, you did not drink, but you're only answer the specific question asked and choosing to ignore the broader implications of the same question.

Rhetorical Errors, in Alphabetical Order

- Ad Hominem Argument
- Appeal to Emotion
- Appeal to False Authority
- Appeal to Ignorance
- Begging the Question
- Dogmatic Argument
- Equivocation
- False Dichotomy
- Faulty Analogies
- Non Sequitur
- Red Herring
- Scare Tactics
- Straw Man Argument

What You'll Be Writing

The three essays included on the AP examination amount to more than half of your total score on the Language and Composition test. While you'll need to be familiar with a wide variety of types of writing, including all of the essay types discussed earlier in this guide, you'll only need to write three types of essays for the test itself:

- One rhetorical analysis or expository essay
- One argumentative essay
- One synthesis essay

These essays differ from work you've done in school in a number of ways. First and foremost, most of your writing experience has been done without significant time pressure. You typically went home, wrote your essay, turned in a rough draft, got it back, revised it and turned it back in over a period of at least several days. If it took two hours to write the initial essay or your first draft wasn't well organized, you had ample opportunities to change your work. Even for in-class essay assignments, like essay questions on a final exam, you're familiar with the material and have the opportunity to study and prepare. Moreover, these essay questions are often less about your ability to write and more about your ability to share information and knowledge gained and retained in class. You and your teacher have a relationship and she knows your writing. You know what is expected. None of this is true about the AP examination.

While we've already introduced how the free response answers are graded, let's look at what makes up a high, average or low-scoring essay response. Recognizing these factors can help you stay on track to an above-average free response score.

- Essays scoring 8-9 are on-topic, answer the essay prompt fully and are well-organized. Examples are logical and relevant, supporting the writer's point. The writer clearly understands the free response passage and engages with it appropriately in the course of their response. They recognize various key points from the passage, in terms of both content and style and integrate these into their response. The essay shows skillful writing and mastery of elements of composition and rhetoric. While the essay does not have to be flawless, errors in grammar or syntax should be minimal and easily overlooked.
- A score of 6-7 reflects a relatively well-organized essay. The examples chosen may be more general than those in a higher scoring essay. While the writer clearly understands the passage and discusses key features, the analysis is not of as high a

quality. The essay is still on-topic, organized, and clear. There may be more errors in grammar and syntax in an essay scoring a 6, rather than a 7.

- A 5 is an average essay or, essentially a C. It's not particularly good, but does address, at least on a surface level, the topic of the passage. Examples are minimal or poorly chosen and the understanding of the passage may be inadequate. The essay is likely not well-organized, does not employ the tools of writing and rhetoric and may have a number of grammar and syntax errors.

- A score of 3-4 suggests that the writer is unable to handle the mechanics of essay writing. The essay only minimally addresses the topic or passage and fails to show an understanding of rhetoric and composition. Organization, grammar and syntax are poor.

- Essays scoring a 1-2 are very poor. The topic has been misunderstood or very poorly handled. There is no discussion of typical components of writing or composition. There is very little or nothing of value in a 1-2 scoring essay.

- A score of 0 or – means the essay does not address the assigned passage or topic or has been left blank.

To break it down, high-scoring essays are clear, appealing to read, and well-thought out. They show that you have actively engaged with the material in the course, topic of the essay and the reading passage for the essay.

While not specifically scored, there are a few other things you can do to improve your overall free response scores. Practicing for the free response questions will give you the opportunity to master these skills. Scoring is subjective and these tips can help you impress your reader and make their job more pleasant.

Write neatly. You can print or write in cursive, but do whichever you feel more comfortable with, rather than what you think you should. While you may occasionally have to scratch out words, limit this as much as possible. Complete thoughts clearly to avoid any hard-to-read continuances or other messiness in your essays. Indent your paragraphs clearly to help the reader recognize the beginning of new paragraphs and create a neat first impression. Keep your paragraphs relatively short and aim to make them approximately the same length. Since scoring is subjective, if your reader isn't struggling with a messy, scribbled up, hard-to-read essay, it's likely to result in an improved score.

Use descriptive, colorful language whenever possible. This will help to keep your reader interested and engaged. An interested reader is more likely to score your essay well. Vary your syntax, sentence length, and rhetorical devices to improve your writing. Avoid repetitive language. If you're unsure how to spell a word or what it means, don't use it.

These are basics of good writing that should come easily to any student after the Language and Composition course, but don't let the time limit allow you to forget them.

Keep length in mind. While this isn't a long essay, it shouldn't be overly short.

Expect to write two to three handwritten pages per question. Essentially, you're aiming for around 400 to 600 words per question. Expect to write a five to six paragraph essay, minimum.

Forget everything you've ever learned about making a good outline. There's no time for that on the Language and Composition test. Your outline should include the bare minimum. A few words can indicate the thesis, followed by a word or two for each paragraph. You can take as many shortcuts as possible in this process. As long as you can decipher what you mean on the outline to keep your essay on track, it's adequate. The key thing to remember is that you only have a few minutes, at most, to plan your free response answers.

Your essay should have a clear introduction and conclusion, along with several body paragraphs. The introduction should state your thesis or main idea clearly and provide your reader with an idea of the content of the essay. Body paragraphs make your argument or illustrate your point, while the conclusion finishes your essay. The topics of your body paragraphs should match the points introduced in the introduction. Keep your conclusion short and to the point.

Each free response question begins with a reading passage and an essay prompt. The essay prompts provide you with a clue to what the readers expect from the essay. You should read the prompt twice. The first time, make certain you understand the type of essay needed. The second time you read the prompt, think carefully about the question and your response to the question. Look for any clues specific to this question, including an author's name, a date, or any possible hints as to the context of this piece or its audience. These clues can help you to organize your thoughts and craft the best possible response. This works for all three essays, but you do need to understand the specifics of the three essays included on the exam; the rhetorical analysis essay, the argumentative essay and the synthesis essay.

The Rhetorical Analysis essay asks you to analyze a passage of writing, particularly the rhetorical tools used in that passage. This essay does not ask you to summarize the passage, but to assess the writing and use of language in the passage. The prompt for this free response question will include words like explain, analyze or point of view. This is an expository essay, in which you are explaining and illustrating something. There's no persuasion, narrative or argument in this essay.

While the rhetorical analysis asks you to analyze someone else's writing in specific and careful detail, the argumentative essay presents your own point-of-view. If you have a great deal of debate experience in your school speech and debate team, you're in luck. You know how to argue a point, and that's exactly what you need to do to succeed. The free response prompt for the argumentative essay includes a specific phrase, "refute, support or qualify". You'll respond to a reading passage with one of these three perspectives. You will support your argument with a variety of examples, specifically, "historical, literary or personal". This essay requires you use the word "I" as you present your own point of view. Since this is your response to a passage, it should be in the present tense, not past, with the exception of a direct discussion of the past. This is, for many students, the easiest and most fun of the three essays.

While the argumentative and rhetorical analysis essays will include only one passage, the synthesis essay requires you to look at multiple passages or sources. This essay is intended to test your ability to look at different information and bring it together into a final essay, as you would for a research paper in college. This is the hardest essay, and you may want to allot most of your 15-minute reading period to these sources, rather than dividing it evenly between the three essays. The prompt will include words like "synthesize" and will also specify how many of the sources you're required to use in your final essay. Read the prompt thoroughly before you tackle the passages. How you read the passages will depend upon your knowledge of the topic. If you know a lot about the passage, you can read much more quickly, carefully noting important points in the text by highlighting or underlining. If you're unfamiliar with the passages, it's more critical that you read carefully. Some of the readings may be only minimally relevant to your essay or may not be relevant at all. Cross off readings you don't plan to use, but don't hesitate to integrate more than the required number of readings. While you have more readings to deal with, you can use the same basic writing strategies for your essay.

You'll have to master each of these essays during your writing process. The next chapter offers you three sample questions; one rhetorical analysis, one argumentative and one synthesis essay. Each essay is accompanied by three possible answers. Based on the standard AP scoring guidelines, one is a high scoring essay and would receive a score of 8 to 9, one is approximately average, or around a 5 or 6. Finally, one essay is poorly written, scoring around a 2-3. Reviewing each of these will allow you to get an idea of what you need to accomplish for the score you want.

From the Second Treatise on Government by John Locke, dating to 1690. Read this philosophical writing and write an essay explaining how Locke used language and rhetoric in his writing.

Sect. 95. MEN being, as has been said, by nature, all free, equal, and independent, no one can be put out of this estate, and subjected to the political power of another, without his own consent. The only way whereby any one divests himself of his natural liberty, and puts on the bonds of civil society, is by agreeing with other men to join and unite into a community for their comfortable, safe, and peaceable living one amongst another, in a secure enjoyment of their properties, and a greater security against any, that are not of it. This any number of men may do, because it injures not the freedom of the rest; they are left as they were in the liberty of the state of nature. When any number of men have so consented to make one community or government, they are thereby presently incorporated, and make one body politic, wherein the majority have a right to act and conclude the rest.

Sect. 96. For when any number of men have, by the consent of every individual, made a community, they have thereby made that community one body, with a power to act as one body, which is only by the will and determination of the majority: for that which acts any community, being only the consent of the individuals of it, and it being necessary to that which is one body to move one way; it is necessary the body should move that way whither the greater force carries it, which is the consent of the majority: or else it is impossible it should act or continue one body, one community, which the consent of every individual that united into it, agreed that it should; and so every one is bound by that consent to be concluded by the majority. And therefore we see, that in assemblies, impowered to act by positive laws, where no number is set by that positive law which impowers them, the act of the majority passes for the act of the whole, and of course determines, as having, by the law of nature and reason, the power of the whole.

Sect. 97. And thus every man, by consenting with others to make one body politic under one government, puts himself under an obligation, to every one of that society, to submit to the determination of the majority, and to be concluded by it; or else this original compact, whereby he with others incorporates into one society, would signify nothing, and be no compact, if he be left free, and under no other ties than he was in before in the state of nature. For what appearance would there be of any compact? what new engagement if he were no farther tied by any decrees of the society, than he himself thought fit, and did actually consent to? This would be still as great a liberty, as he himself had before his compact, or any one else in the state of nature hath, who may submit himself, and consent to any acts of it if he thinks fit.

Sect. 98. For if the consent of the majority shall not, in reason, be received as the act of the whole, and conclude every individual; nothing but the consent of every individual can make any thing to be the act of the whole: but such a consent is next to impossible ever to be had, if we consider the infirmities of health, and avocations of business, which in a number, though much less than that of a commonwealth, will necessarily keep many away from the public assembly. To which if we add the variety of opinions, and contrariety of interests, which unavoidably happen in all collections of men, the coming into society upon such terms would be only like Cato's coming into the theatre, only to go out again. Such a constitution as this would make the mighty Leviathan of a shorter duration, than the feeblest creatures, and not let it outlast the day it was born in: which cannot be supposed, till we can think, that rational creatures should desire and constitute societies only to be dissolved: for where the majority cannot conclude the rest, there they cannot act as one body, and consequently will be immediately dissolved again.

Sect. 99. Whosoever therefore out of a state of nature unite into a community, must be understood to give up all the power, necessary to the ends for which they unite into society, to the majority of the community, unless they expresly agreed in any number greater than the majority. And this is done by barely agreeing to unite into one political society, which is all the compact that is, or needs be, between the individuals, that enter into, or make up a commonwealth. And thus that, which begins and actually constitutes any political society, is nothing but the consent of any number of freemen capable of a majority to unite and incorporate into such a society. And this is that, and that only, which did, or could give beginning to any lawful government in the world.

Low Scoring Rhetorical Analysis

John Locke wrote about freedom and equality. He is concerned with how free and equal people come together to form a free society. He uses the tools of rhetoric in his writing to convince his reader that people are free and equal.

Locke relies upon ethos, or his own thoughts, as the basis for his argument. He is a well-educated man and able to write about the freedom of men. His interest in free will requires that he rely on himself, not someone else for authority. He uses long sentences to make himself sound smarter.

He classifies his work, separating it in to sections. The sections are organized by topic. He compares a voluntary society and laws agreed to to the state of nature. He thinks the state of nature, or man without government, is better than an organized government. The state of nature is how man lives without laws or community.

Locke wants people to form communities through free will, not because they have to or are forced to. Everyone has to agree to be a part of the community and agree to government laws. He does opt for clear language and uses examples to illustrate his argument. This is a work of non-fiction, so he doesn't use figurative language. He classifies and organizes his work into sections, but does not make comparisons. His argument doesn't contain any rhetorical errors.

John Locke's work supports free government or even democracy. He creates a philosophical discussion supporting his notion of government and society, based upon a belief in free will. He relies upon his own authority, rather than logic or appeals to emotion for his discussion. Locke's work must have been convincing, since democracy ended up being the best form of government.

An Average Essay

John Locke's Second Treatise on Government presents a skilled argument for the existence of free will and consensual government, based upon mutual agreement. Locke's writing is convincing, incorporating a number of aspects of traditional rhetoric, including figurative language, comparisons, and examples. This short excerpt shows his intelligence and illustrates his importance as a political thinker.

Locke compares the existence of a voluntary community or government to man in a state of nature, free of government or laws. While the state of nature is, according to Locke, superior, a voluntary society is an acceptable alternative. Laws are developed by the people and agreed to by the people. Free will is essential for the existence of Locke's free society. Everyone must choose to comply with the laws and regulations in order for the government to function.

He uses examples to support his argument, illustrating his defense of a free government and how such a community would work. He explains the process of assemblies, allowing the majority to rule and make decisions for the community. He defends his communal government by noting that those who do not wish to join in may be left free to live as they choose, free from the laws and regulations of these communities. It appears that Locke supports a local form of government, rather than envisioning something larger, like a national government. He does believe that joining in government forces the individual to choose to give up some rights in favor of the whole.

Locke uses figurative language in his writing. He compares the free and voluntary society to a Leviathan, or a sea monster. The Leviathan is stronger than the individual. He compares the individual in government to a Roman theater. This figurative language helps the reader to understand his view of government.

John Locke does not attempt to appeal to emotion or pathos. He attempts to provide the reader with a logical argument based upon his own authority and intellect. His discussions of government, like the Second Treatise on Government, helped to inspire later governments, focused on the rule of the majority, led by assemblies. Individuals within the community had the ability to make choices and have a say in the role of their governments and societies. Locke's use of language and rhetoric helps to support his argument and convince the reader of the value of this sort of society, rather than an absolute or constitutional monarchy.

A High Scoring Essay

John Locke's Second Treatise on Government illustrates the essential importance of rhetoric and language in works of persuasive non-fiction. Locke presents an argument in defense of democratic government, led by the majority. He relies upon a number of different rhetorical tools in his discussion, including ethos or authority, comparison, figurative language, and analogy. While the lasting political influence of Locke's writing is undeniable, his rhetorical skill contributed to his importance and historical relevance.

Locke uses upon both his own authority and divine authority in this text from the late 17th century. As a philosopher, he was a learned man and could produce a thoughtful and logical argument, but as a man in a religious era, divine authority proved even more critical to his discussion. Divine authority, including references to free will as a biblical principle, supported and gave credence to Locke's discussion of community, society and government. While today, ethos might be the result of education or other credentials, in Locke's time, the highest authority, or ethos, was from God.

During the course of his work, Locke compares a voluntary society or government to the state of nature. The state of nature is man living without government. In the state of nature, choices are made on an individual basis, rather than a communal one. In joining together to form a community, one gives up some fundamental rights present in the state of nature. This comparison provides insights into the benefits of community, but also the sacrifices that come with choosing to live together and form a majority government.

John Locke uses figurative language and analogies to make clear how government must function. If a government cannot be ruled by the majority, it would be like Cato entering the theatre and leaving, or accomplishing nothing at all. A government that can accomplish nothing would turn the Leviathan, or constitution, into something utterly weak. Only through acceptance of majority rule, or sacrificing the personal rights associated with the state of nature, can the society or community survive and continue. The simile, or comparison to Cato's actions, suggests the possible futility of government, while the analogy comparing the constitution to the Leviathan helps the reader to comprehend, in clear and concrete terms, the necessity of legal, majority rule.

According to Locke, government begins with an act of free will on the part of the individual. These individuals agree, of their own choice, acting independently, to join together to form a community. Together, they look out for one another and act for the greater good of the whole. In this, the needs of the majority must, at least some of the time, outweigh the will and desires of the individual. Locke's argument is familiar to the modern reader, but it was new to the reader of the 17th century. Through language and rhetoric, Locke made his argument on the basis of divine authority and free will as given by God. His use of comparisons, including both the comparison between government and the state of nature, and broader comparisons and analogies helps to make the abstract ideal of government and majority rule graspable and concrete for the reader.

Argumentative Essay Sample Question and Answers

This short excerpt, taken from a 19th century text on etiquette, offers a discussion of honesty. Your argumentative essay should refute, support or qualify this text and interpretation of honesty and politeness.:

"Many persons plead a love of truth as an apology for rough manners, as if truth was never gentle and kind, but always harsh, morose, and forbidding. Surely good manners and a good conscience are no more inconsistent with each other than beauty and innocence, which are strikingly akin, and always look the better for companionship. Roughness and honesty are indeed sometimes found together in the same person, but he is a poor judge of human nature who takes ill-manners to be a guarantee of probity of character. Some persons object to politeness, that its language is unmeaning and false. But this is easily answered. A lie is not locked up in a phrase, but must exist, if at all, in the mind of the speaker. In the ordinary compliments of civilized life, there is no intention to deceive, and consequently no falsehood. Polite language is pleasant to the ear, and soothing to the heart, while rough words are just the reverse; and if not the product of ill temper, are very apt to produce it. The plainest of truths, let it be remembered, can be conveyed in civil speech, while the most malignant lies may find utterance, and often do, in the language of the fishmarket."

Low Scoring Argumentative Essay

I think you should always be honest, even if it hurts people's feelings. Honestly is always the best policy. If you're not honest, people could end up feeling even more sad or hurt than if you are.

Once, I told my friend she looked fat in her dress. I was honest, even though it made her sad. She wore a different dress and looked better. It was better that I was honest with her in that situation, even though it wasn't nice. She went out looking good and forgave me for being honest. Isn't that ironic?

In stories, choosing to lie leads to bad things happening. In Peter and the Wolf, Peter lied for attention, then didn't get help when he needed it. If Peter had been honest that he didn't want to watch the sheep, he would have gotten help when he needed it. Being honest could have saved the sheep from the wolf.

When I was a kid, my mom told me I had to always be polite about presents. Even if I didn't like them, I was supposed to say thank you and pretend I did. This led to me getting presents I didn't like over & over again, because the person giving the present thought I liked it. Being honest might have hurt their feelings, but I'd have gotten better presents.

The writer says you can be polite and honest, but sometimes I don't think you can or should have to be. If you can be nice and be honest, it's good, like I could tell my friend the other dress looked better, rather than that the first one looked bad, that's good. When you can't be both nice and honest, you should always be honest.

Average Scoring Argumentative Essay

Honesty is an essential value, but politeness and good manners help all of us to function in society. Surprisingly, these two aren't necessarily opposed, even if they're sometimes a hard combination. Literally, combining honesty and good manners can help you to succeed in work, life and relationships. Even so, politeness can be more important than honesty sometimes.

The author states that a lie requires intent to deceive. If there is no intent to deceive, there is no dishonesty. For instance, if you ask how I am and I respond that I am fine, my response if polite. You and I are both aware that the question is asked for reasons of etiquette and my answer, that I am fine, in no way really speaks to my health or well-being. On the other hand, if you're a close friend and ask about a problem and I say it's fine, I may well intend to deceive you and be dishonest. Politeness may, sometimes, allow for these little white lies, but as there is no intent to deceive, these aren't really lies and cause no harm.

You can also maintain kindness and good manners while being at least mostly honest, even if it sometimes is rather difficult. If you need to end a relationship, you may have to tell the truth. You can, however, soften the blow with politeness. For instance, you might say "it's not you, it's me" or blame outside responsibilities as a way to avoid saying that you really don't like someone. These statements are more polite than true, but are done to save hurt feelings and reduce sadness, so it's better than the alternative.

We also offer up polite lies at other times, with the intent to deceive. You might, for instance, make an excuse to avoid an invitation or say you liked a gift you thought was awful. You do intend to deceive the listener, but again the reason is to reduce harm for them and it may be more polite to explain that you have another invitation rather than announce that you'd rather stay home than go to her party.

If you can be both honest and polite, you should be. You could, for instance, be honest with your grandmother about the unwanted gift and explain that you so appreciated the sweater, but it wasn't quite your color and you exchanged it for a pair of slippers you adore, or you could simply tell her how grateful you are that she thought of you on your birthday. This is better than lying, when you can. Sometimes, though "civil speech," to quote the passage, isn't enough to cover up brutal honesty.

Sometimes it's simply good manners to tell a little or not-so-little white lie. These social lies help to avoid hurt feelings, smooth over awkward situations, and reduce stress. You're not lying about anything important or lying to make things better for yourself, so it's okay to lie if you have to to be polite and can't be both honest and polite.

A High Scoring Argumentative Essay

Those who earn the greatest respect are both honest and kind, both in the small interactions of everyday life in school, work or relationships and in broader relationships between companies and even nations. Dishonesty rarely improves the situation, but neither does coarseness and rudeness, even when honest. While honesty can be brutal, it does not have to be. Good manners, etiquette and politeness can help one to be both honest and thoughtful. As the author states, "the plainest of truths" can be conveyed with civil speech and kindness. There is no need, in pursuit of honesty and truthfulness, to be unkind, rude or coarse.

Courtesy and kindness can, in the everyday, make an embarrassing situation less so. Once, at an academic event, someone quietly told me that the back of my skirt was caught in my tights. I blushed furiously, but thanked her profusely. It was far better to be told this in private than have it become public. Her honesty, combined with discretion and good manners, saved me public disgrace.

Even socially awkward situations that require a delicate hand can be saved by this combination of good manners and honesty. If asked a simple question, you often have more than two choices for your answer. For instance, if you're reviewing a friend's paper and it's, quite frankly, rather poorly written, you could, honestly, say it was awful. You could, on the other hand, opt to praise their organization and spelling, but mention that you were concerned about their grammar and the subject matter chosen. Both of these are honest responses, but one will result in a much more positive interaction, overall.

On a much more substantial scale, international diplomacy requires a combination of honesty and good manners, sometimes, in this case, called tact. One country may censure another, issuing a statement questioning their actions; however, coarse language or personal insults are carefully avoided to reduce the risk of offense. The United States, for instance, is sending a delegation to the Sochi Olympics in 2014; this is an example, in a diplomatic sense of good manners. The President and First Lady will not be part of the delegation, revealing the honest disagreement with Russian political policies. It would have caused a more significant diplomatic incident for the United States to refuse to send a delegation to the Olympics, but would have been dishonest to send the usual delegation, complete with high-ranking politicians.

To paraphrase Mary Poppins, "a spoonful of sugar makes the medicine go down". Politeness and kindness are, in the pursuit of honesty, the sugar that makes the medicine, or honesty, a bit more palatable. This is true both in the smallest of everyday interactions and much more significant ones. You can temper honesty, even when it must be rather blunt, with kindness. This helps to raise up those around you, rather than tearing them down and encourages them to open their minds to your words, supporting positive change.

These readings all focus on the subject of crime, particularly murder. Consider the insights and perspectives of these writings to synthesize them and bring them together in a single essay on the subject of murder in the 19th century. Use at least two of the four sources in your essay.

Passion, when it once gains an ascendant over our minds, is often more fatal to us than the most deliberate course of vice could be. On every little start it throws us from the paths of reason, and hurries us in one moment into acts more wicked and more dangerous than we could at any other time suffer to enter our imagination. As anger is justly said to be a short madness, so, while the frenzy is upon us, blood is shed as easily as water, and the mind is so filled with fury that there is no room left for compassion. There cannot be a stronger proof of what I have been observing than in the unhappy end of the poor woman who is the subject of this chapter.

Jane Griffin was the daughter of honest and substantial parents, who educated her with very great tenderness and care, particularly with respect to religion, in which she was well and rationally instructed. As she grew up her person grew agreeable, and she had a lively wit and a very tolerable share of understanding. She lived with a very good reputation, and to general satisfaction, in several places, till she married Mr. Griffin, who kept the Three Pigeons in Smithfield[2].

She behaved herself so well and was so obliging in her house that she drew to it a very great trade, in which she managed so as to leave everyone well satisfied. Yet she allowed her temper to fly out into sudden gusts of passion, and that folly alone sullied her character to those who were witnesses of it, and at last caused a shameful end to an honest and industrious life.

One Elizabeth Osborn, coming to live with her as a servant, she proved of a disposition as Mrs. Griffin could by no means agree with. They were continually differing and having high words, in which, as is usual on such occasions, Mrs. Griffin made use of wild expressions, which though she might mean nothing by them when she spoke them, yet proved of the utmost ill consequence, after the fatal accident of the maid's death. For being then given in evidence, they were esteemed proofs of malice prepense, which ought to be a warning to all hasty people to endeavour at some restraint upon their tongues when in fits of anger, since we are not only sure of answering hereafter for every idle word we speak, but even here they may, as in this case, become fatal in the last degree.

It was said at the time those things were transacted that jealousy was in some degree the source of their debates, but of that I can affirm nothing. It no way appeared as to the accident which immediately drew on her death, and which happened after this manner.

One evening, having cut some cold fowl for the children's supper, it happened the key of the cellar was missing on a sudden, and on Mrs. Griffin's first speaking of it they began to look for it. But it not being found, Mrs. Griffin went into the room where the maid was, and using some very harsh expression, taxed her with having seen it, or laid it out of the way. Instead of excusing herself modestly, the maid flew out also into ill language at her mistress, and in the midst of the fray, the knife with which she had been cutting lying unluckily by her, she snatched it up, and stuck it into the maid's bosom; her stays happening to be unluckily open, it entered so deep as to give her a mortal wound.

After she had struck her Mrs. Griffin went upstairs, not imagining that she had killed her, but the alarm was soon raised on her falling down, and Mrs. Griffin was carried before a magistrate, and committed to Newgate. When she was first confined, she seemed hopeful of getting off at her trial, yet though she did not make any confession, she was very sorrowful and concerned. As her trial drew nearer, her apprehensions grew stronger, till notwithstanding all she could urge in her defence, the jury found her guilty, and sentence was pronounced as the Law directs.

I was at the time, and still am, a professor in that city and university which had the melancholy distinction of being its theater. I knew familiarly all the parties who were concerned in it, either as sufferers or as agents. I was present from first to last, and watched the whole course of the mysterious storm which fell upon our devoted city in a strength like that of a West Indian hurricane, and which did seriously threaten at one time to depopulate our university, through the dark suspicions which settled upon its members, and the natural reaction of generous indignation in repelling them; while the city in its more stationary and native classes would very soon have manifested THEIR awful sense of things, of the hideous insecurity for life, and of the unfathomable dangers which had undermined their hearths below their very feet, by sacrificing, whenever circumstances allowed them, their houses and beautiful gardens in exchange for days uncursed by panic, and nights unpolluted by blood. Nothing, I can take upon myself to assert, was left undone of all that human foresight could suggest, or human ingenuity could accomplish. But observe the melancholy result: the more certain did these arrangements strike people as remedies for the evil, so much the more effectually did they aid the terror, but, above all, the awe, the sense of mystery, when ten cases of total extermination, applied to separate households, had occurred, in every one of which these precautionary aids had failed to yield the slightest assistance. The horror, the perfect frenzy of fear, which seized upon the town after that experience, baffles all attempt at description. Had these various contrivances failed merely in some human and intelligible way, as by bringing the aid too tardily— still, in such cases, though the danger would no less have been evidently deepened, nobody would have felt any further mystery than what, from the very first, rested upon the persons and the motives of the murderers. But, as it was, when, in ten separate cases of exterminating carnage, the astounded police, after an examination the most searching, pursued from day to day, and almost exhausting the patience by the minuteness of the investigation, had finally pronounced that no attempt apparently had been made to benefit by any of the signals preconcerted, that no footstep apparently had moved in that direction—then, and after that result, a blind misery of fear fell upon the population, so much the worse than any anguish of a beleaguered city that is awaiting the storming fury of a victorious enemy, by how much the shadowy, the uncertain, the infinite, is at all times more potent in mastering the mind than a danger that is known, measurable, palpable, and human. The very police, instead of offering protection or encouragement, were seized with terror for themselves. And the general feeling, as it was described to me by a grave citizen whom I met in a morning walk (for the overmastering sense of a public calamity broke down every barrier of reserve, and all men talked freely to all men in the streets, as they would have done during the rockings of an earthquake), was, even among the boldest, like that which sometimes takes possession of the mind in dreams—when one feels oneself sleeping alone, utterly divided from all call or hearing of friends, doors open that should be shut, or unlocked that should be triply secured, the very walls gone, barriers swallowed up by unknown abysses, nothing around one but frail curtains, and a world of illimitable night, whisperings at a distance, correspondence going on between darkness and darkness, like one deep calling to another, and the dreamer's own heart the center from which the whole network of this unimaginable chaos radiates, by means of which the blank PRIVATIONS of silence and darkness become powers the most POSITIVE and awful.

The difficulties surrounding the theory of retribution have led to other definitions of punishment. Punishment, it is said, is not inflicted on the offender as a retribution for his misdeeds, it is inflicted for the purpose of protecting society against its enemies. Such a view leaves moral considerations entirely out of account; it leaves no room for the just indignation of the public at the spectacle of crime. It is defective in other ways. For instance, a criminal has a particular animosity against some single individual; it may be he murders this person, or does him grievous bodily harm. Such an offender has no similar animosity against any one else; as far as the rest of the community is concerned he is perfectly harmless. On the supposition that punishment is only intended to protect society against the criminal, a man of this description would escape punishment altogether. Or supposing a man (and this often happens), after committing some serious crime for which he is sent to penal servitude, sincerely and bitterly repented of it, and would be, if released, a perfectly harmless member of the community, such a man, according to the theory we are now discussing, should be released at once. The certainty that the public conscience would tolerate no such step shows that punishment has a wider object than the mere attainment of social security.

Punishment is only a means say some; its real end is the reformation of the offender. The practical application of such a principle would lead to very astonishing results. It is perfectly well known that there is no more incorrigible set of offenders than habitual vagrants and drunkards. And on the other hand, the most easily reformed of all offenders is often some person who has committed a serious crime under circumstances which could not possibly recur. According to the theory that reformation is the only end of punishment, petty offenders would be shut up all their lives, while the perpetrator of a grave crime would soon be set free. An absurd result of this kind is fatal to the pretention that punishment is merely a means and not also an end.

Is it the end of punishment to act as a deterrent? We are often told from the judicial bench that a man receives a certain sentence as a warning and example to others. If such is the end of punishment it lamentably fails in its purpose, for in a number of cases it neither deters the offender nor the class from which the offender springs. It was under the influence of this idea that criminals used to be hanged in public, but experience failed to show that these ghastly exhibitions had much deterrent effect on the community. Besides, it is rather ridiculous to say, I do not punish you for the crime you have committed, I punish you as a warning to others. In these circumstances the effect of punishment is not to be upon the person punished, but upon a third party who has not fallen into crime. Unless the punishment is just in itself, society has no right to inflict it in the hope of scaring others from criminal courses. Justice administered in this spirit, turns the convicted offender into a whipping boy; the punishment ceases to be related to the offence, and is merely related to the effect it will have on a certain circle of spectators.

In our view, punishment ought to be regarded as at once an expiation and a discipline, or, in other words, an expiatory discipline. This definition includes all that is valuable in the theories just reviewed, and excludes all that is imperfect in them. The criminal is an offender against the fundamental order of society in somewhat the same way as a disobedient child is an offender against the centre of authority in the home or the school. The punishment inflicted on the child may take the form of revenge, or it may take the form of retribution, or it may take the form of deterrence, but it undoubtedly takes its highest form when it combines expiation with discipline. Punishment of this nature still remains punitive as it ought to do, but it is at the same time a kind of punishment from which something may be learned. It does not merely consist in inflicting pain, although the presence of this element is essential to its efficacy; it consists rather in inflicting pain in such a way as will tend to discipline and reform the character. Such a conception of punishment excludes the barbarous element of vengeance; it is based upon the civilised ideas of justice and humanity, or rather upon the sentiment of justice alone, for justice is never truly just except when its tendency is also to humanise.

The editor here proceeds to argue that the body must have been in the water "not three days merely, but, at least, five times three days," because it was so far decomposed that Beauvais had great difficulty in recognizing it. This latter point, however, was fully disproved. I continue the translation:

"What, then, are the facts on which M. Beauvais says that he has no doubt the body was that of Marie Rogæt? He ripped up the gown sleeve, and says he found marks which satisfied him of the identity. The public generally supposed those marks to have consisted of some description of scars. He rubbed the arm and found hair upon it—something as indefinite, we think, as can readily be imagined—as little conclusive as finding an arm in the sleeve. M. Beauvais did not return that night, but sent word to Madame Rogæt, at seven o'clock, on Wednesday evening, that an investigation was still in progress respecting her daughter. If we allow that Madame Rogæt, from her age and grief, could not go over, (which is allowing a great deal,) there certainly must have been some one who would have thought it worth while to go over and attend the investigation, if they thought the body was that of Marie. Nobody went over. There was nothing said or heard about the matter in the Rue Pavæe St. Andræe, that reached even the occupants of the same building. M. St. Eustache, the lover and intended husband of Marie, who boarded in her mother's house, deposes that he did not hear of the discovery of the body of his intended until the next morning, when M. Beauvais came into his chamber and told him of it. For an item of news like this, it strikes us it was very coolly received."

In this way the journal endeavored to create the impression of an apathy on the part of the relatives of Marie, inconsistent with the supposition that these relatives believed the corpse to be hers. Its insinuations amount to this:—that Marie, with the connivance of her friends, had absented herself from the city for reasons involving a charge against her chastity; and that these friends, upon the discovery of a corpse in the Seine, somewhat resembling that of the girl, had availed themselves of the opportunity to impress the public with the belief of her death. But L'Etoile was again over-hasty. It was distinctly proved that no apathy, such as was imagined, existed; that the old lady was exceedingly feeble, and so agitated as to be unable to attend to any duty, that St. Eustache, so far from receiving the news coolly, was distracted with grief, and bore himself so frantically, that M. Beauvais prevailed upon a friend and relative to take charge of him, and prevent his attending the examination at the disinterment. Moreover, although it was stated by L'Etoile, that the corpse was re-interred at the public expense—that an advantageous offer of private sculpture was absolutely declined by the family—and that no member of the family attended the ceremonial:—although, I say, all this was asserted by L'Etoile in furtherance of the impression it designed to convey—yet all this was satisfactorily disproved. In a subsequent number of the paper, an attempt was made to throw suspicion upon Beauvais himself. The editor says:

"Now, then, a change comes over the matter. We are told that on one occasion, while a Madame B—— was at Madame Rogæt's house, M. Beauvais, who was going out, told her that a gendarme was expected there, and she, Madame B., must not say anything to the gendarme until he returned, but let the matter be for him.... In the present posture of affairs, M. Beauvais appears to have the whole matter locked up in his head. A single step cannot be taken without M. Beauvais; for, go which way you will, you run against him.... For some reason, he determined that nobody shall have any thing to do with the proceedings but himself, and he has elbowed the male relatives out of the way, according to their representations, in a very singular manner. He seems to have been very much averse to permitting the relatives to see the body."

By the following fact, some color was given to the suspicion thus thrown upon Beauvais. A visitor at his office, a few days prior to the girl's disappearance, and during the absence of its occupant, had observed a rose in the key-hole of the door, and the name "Marie" inscribed upon a slate which hung near at hand.

The general impression, so far as we were enabled to glean it from the newspapers, seemed to be, that Marie had been the victim of a gang of desperadoes—that by these she had been borne across the river, maltreated and murdered. Le Commerciel, (*11) however, a print of extensive influence, was earnest in combating this popular idea. I quote a passage or two from its columns:

"We are persuaded that pursuit has hitherto been on a false scent, so far as it has been directed to the Barriære du Roule. It is impossible that a person so well known to thousands as this young woman was, should have passed three blocks without some one having seen her; and any one who saw her would have remembered it, for she interested all who knew her. It was when the streets were full of people, when she went out.... It is impossible that she could have gone to the Barriære du Roule, or to the Rue des Dræmes, without being recognized by a dozen persons; yet no one has come forward who saw her outside of her mother's door, and there is no evidence, except the testimony concerning her expressed intentions, that she did go out at all. Her gown was torn, bound round her, and tied; and by that the body was carried as a bundle. If the murder had been committed at the Barriære du Roule, there would have been no necessity for any such arrangement. The fact that the body was found floating near the Barriære, is no proof as to where it was thrown into the water..... A piece of one of the unfortunate girl's petticoats, two feet long and one foot wide, was torn out and tied under her chin around the back of her head, probably to prevent screams. This was done by fellows who had no pocket-handkerchief."

A day or two before the Prefect called upon us, however, some important information reached the police, which seemed to overthrow, at least, the chief portion of Le Commerciel's argument. Two small boys, sons of a Madame Deluc, while roaming among the woods near the Barriære du Roule, chanced to penetrate a close thicket, within which were three or four large stones, forming a kind of seat, with a back and footstool. On the upper stone lay a white petticoat; on the second a silk scarf. A parasol, gloves, and a pocket-handkerchief were also here found. The handkerchief bore the name "Marie Rogæt." Fragments of dress were discovered on the brambles around. The earth was trampled, the bushes were broken, and there was every evidence of a struggle. Between the thicket and the river, the fences were found taken down, and the ground bore evidence of some heavy burthen having been dragged along it.

A weekly paper, Le Soleil,(*12) had the following comments upon this discovery—comments which merely echoed the sentiment of the whole Parisian press:

"The things had all evidently been there at least three or four weeks; they were all mildewed down hard with the action of the rain and stuck together from mildew. The grass had grown around and over some of them. The silk on the parasol was strong, but the threads of it were run together within. The upper part, where it had been doubled and folded, was all mildewed and rotten, and tore on its being opened..... The pieces of her frock torn out by the bushes were about three inches wide and six inches long. One part was the hem of the frock, and it had been mended; the other piece was part of the skirt, not the hem. They looked like strips torn off, and were on the thorn bush, about a foot from the ground..... There can be no doubt, therefore, that the spot of this appalling outrage has been discovered."

A Low Scoring Synthesis Essay

Murder first became a real problem in the 19th century and they had to look for a solution to punishment for murder. Punishment served to prevent crime, but also to, theoretically, teach the criminal not to do it again. Jails were used for punishment, but they also executed people. Executing people doesn't teach them anything since they're already dead.

If punishment is a deterrent, or something that prevents something else, executing criminals should stop murder. The other passages show that murders still happened, even if criminals were executed for them. Therefore, executing people didn't deter other people from committing murder. This might be because murders were crimes of passion, without any planning.

So, since punishment doesn't prevent anything, does it teach the criminal anything? Criminals were often executed in the 19th century, so they couldn't learn anything from it. Executing them did prevent them from committing more crimes, but didn't stop others from committing crimes. The author suggests that punishment should hurt, but help to reform the criminal. This only applies to crimes other than murder. Murderers weren't sent to jail or reformed.

The other passages are stories about specific murders or people's reactions to murder. They show that murders were happening regardless of punishment. Punishment did, maybe, make society feel better. This is vengeance though, and didn't really help the victim of crime or the rest of society. If a murderer was caught and executed, people didn't have to be afraid that they would be murdered, at least until the next murderer came along.

These readings show that crime isn't a modern phenomenon. People were murdered in the past too and were punished for murder, when they could catch the criminal. Some criminals, like Jack the Ripper, weren't caught at all because the police weren't very good. Punishment wasn't very useful at all. It didn't stop other criminals from committing crime and didn't prevent murder, even back then. `

An Average Synthesis Essay

Issues of crime and punishment are not new in the 20th and 21st century. Crimes, including property crimes and even murder, were common in the 19th century as well. Society tried to understand the reasons for crime and how to prevent crime and punish criminals. Even so, everyone was interested in dark and scary stories, like those of murder.

The first passage describes a straightforward crime of passion. The author is even somewhat sympathetic to the killer. She's a woman from a good family, well-raised, and normally, perfectly nice. She just has a bad temper and accidentally killed someone in a fit of rage. This is, to the reader, somewhat more understandable. We later read about the response of society to a rash of especially violent murders. Unlike the story of Jane Griffin, these are hard to understand and outside the range of normal comprehension. While the story of Mary Roget is about the body and the investigation, there is no sign that this was a crime of passion, recognizable to the reader.

Both the story of Jane Griffin and the excerpt from Thomas de Quincey were intended for the average reader. They showed how interested people were in reading about murder, even if it was scary. The same is true of Poe's story about the murder of Mary Roget. These stories show that even the uptight people of the 19th century had a dark side and were interested in murder, just like we are today. These stories aren't all that different from a serial killer documentary or website.

Two of these three passages are written to make them seem even scarier and harder to comprehend. Thomas de Quincey and Poe both wanted to frighten their readers. While the passage about Jane Griffin is relatively straightforward, Poe and de Quincey use more literary and figurative language. They were based on true occurrences, but like horror films, appealed because they were scary. Like a made-for-tv movie based on a true story, Poe and de Quincey made reality into something even more frightening than it really was, making the individual personally aware of the risk and reality of murder.

While most of us would acknowledge that murder is treated as entertainment today, with television movies and novels, this isn't a new phenomenon. Even in the 19th century, stories about murder drew in readers, encouraging them to buy books, magazines and newspapers. This interest wasn't always simply educational. While the story of Jane Griffin is journalistic and straightforward, the passages by de Quincey and Poe are not. These passages show that stories of murder were moving from the front page of the newspaper to the world of the novel and the short story, and eventually movies and television.

A High Scoring Synthesis Essay

The darkest parts of the human soul have long been fascinating to both readers and writers. Murder sells newspapers, books, and today, television and movies. The modern desire for shows like CSI clearly is not new. These writings, including the story of Jane Griffin, de Quincey's discussion of the response to murder and Edgar Allen Poe's Mary Roget all reveal a 19th century interest in both murder and the response to murder. The idea of murder provokes fear, whether we recognize ourselves in the face of the murderer, in the frightened crowd, or in the interested investigator.

All of these authors are sharing a story, referencing current or recent events, and creating an impression in the mind of the reader. The author of the Jane Griffin story is presenting her story without great drama; however, he is sympathetic to the killer. We know nothing of Jane's victim, other than her social status. De Quincey is unconcerned with the facts of murder, but dramatically focuses on the public and police response to that murder. He draws in his reader with a strong dark tone, emphasizing the atmosphere of fear created by the murders in the community. Finally, Poe's interest in the case of Mary Roget is critical and investigative. He is less concerned with either the victim or the criminal than with the circumstances of the investigation, in essence, asking the reader to try to solve the case and piece together the clues. Together, these three form a complete and compelling look into the story of murder in the 19th century.

The 19th century brought media to the masses. Literacy rates were increasing, newspapers were cheap, and information travelled more quickly than it ever had before. While murders certainly happened before the 19th century, both as crimes of passion and killings that seemed darker and more random, these could largely pass relatively unknown. They were not the beginnings of mass hysteria, as recounted by De Quincey. Only access to information, to the crime scene, to the newspapers, could create that. With that access came a new interest in what had happened and the story behind it, including the story of the investigation, like that told by Poe in Mary Roget.

While each of these works presents a different view of crime, none of them are truly objective or journalistic. The authors did not have access to the facts, and where needed, were willing to create their own for the sake of the story. They were not attempting to create an accurate narrative about murder. Instead, they wrote stories to entice and entertain the reader. The reader was invited to imagine the chaos and fear in the wake of murder or to criticize the incomplete investigation by the police force. The readers could, in this, feel themselves better than the characters in their story. While they might be frightened and entertained, at no point do any of these authors ask the reader to consider themselves in the place of the victim. That, it seems, is too frightening a possibility.

These works all sit on the cusp of a new era in crime, murder, and even the fictional stories of murder and crime. By the early 20th century, new technology would change criminal investigation, and along with it, help to create new stories about murder, both literary and journalistic. These three passages show us that the readers of the 19th century were already interested in murder as a genre, both in fictionalized and non-fiction representations.

Practice Test 1

Cecil B. Hartley.   The Gentleman's Book of Etiquette and Manual of Politeness.

1   "We now come to habits at table, which are very important. However agreeable a man may

2   be in society, if he offends or disgusts by his table traits, he will soon be scouted from it, and

3   justly so. There are some broad rules for behavior at table. Whenever there is a servant to

4   help you, never help yourself. Never put a knife into your mouth, not even with cheese,

5   which should be eaten with a fork. Never use a spoon for anything but liquids. Never touch

6   anything edible with your fingers.

7   "Forks were, undoubtedly, a later invention than fingers, but, as we are not cannibals, I am

8   inclined to think they were a good one. There are some few things which you may take up

9   with your fingers. Thus an epicure will eat even macaroni with his fingers; and as sucking

10   asparagus is more pleasant than chewing it, you may, as an epicure, take it up *au naturel*.

11   But both these things are generally eaten with a fork. Bread is, of course, eaten with the

12   fingers, and it would be absurd to carve it with your knife and fork. It must, on the contrary,

13   always be broken when not buttered, and you should never put a slice of dry bread to your

14   mouth to bite a piece off. Most fresh fruit, too, is eaten with the natural prongs, but when

15   you have peeled an orange or apple, you should cut it with the aid of the fork, unless you

16   can succeed in breaking it. Apropos of which, I may hint that no epicure ever yet put a knife

17   to an apple, and that an orange should be peeled with a spoon. But the art of peeling an

18   orange so as to hold its own juice, and its own sugar too, is one that can scarcely be taught

19   in a book.

20   "However, let us go to dinner, and I will soon tell you whether you are a well-bred man or

21   not; and here let me premise that what is good manners for a small dinner is good manners

22   for a large one, and *vice versa*. Now, the first thing you do is to sit down. Stop, sir! pray do

23   not cram yourself into the table in that way; no, nor sit a yard from it, like that. How

24   graceless, inconvenient, and in the way of conversation! Why, dear me! you are positively

25   putting your elbows on the table, and now you have got your hands fumbling about with

26   the spoons and forks, and now you are nearly knocking my new hock glasses over. Can't you

27   take your hands down, sir? Didn't you learn that in the nursery? Didn't your mamma say to

28   you, 'Never put your hands above the table except to carve or eat?' Oh! but come, no

29   nonsense, sit up, if you please. I can't have your fine head of hair forming a side dish on my

30   table; you must not bury your face in the plate, you came to show it, and it ought to be

31   alive. Well, but there is no occasion to throw your head back like that, you look like an

32 alderman, sir, **after** dinner. Pray, don't lounge in that sleepy way. You are here to eat,
33 drink, and be merry. You can sleep when you get home.

34 "Well, then, I suppose you can see your napkin. Got none, indeed! Very likely, in **my** house.
35 You may be sure that I never sit down to a meal without napkins. I don't want to make my
36 tablecloths unfit for use, and I don't want to make my trousers unwearable. Well, now, we
37 are all seated, you can unfold it on your knees; no, no; don't tuck it into your waistcoat like
38 an alderman; and what! what on earth do you mean by wiping your forehead with it? Do
39 you take it for a towel? Well, never mind, I am consoled that you did not go farther, and use
40 it as a pocket-handkerchief. So talk away to the lady on your right, and wait till soup is
41 handed to you. By the way, that waiting is the most important part of table manners, and,
42 as much as possible, you should avoid asking for anything or helping yourself from the
43 table. Your soup you eat with a spoon—I don't know what else you **could** eat it with—but
44 then it must be one of good size. Yes, that will do, but I beg you will not make that odious
45 noise in drinking your soup. It is louder than a dog lapping water, and a cat would be quite
46 genteel to it. Then you need not scrape up the plate in that way, nor even tilt it to get the
47 last drop. I shall be happy to send you some more; but I must just remark, that it is not the
48 custom to take two helpings of soup, and it is liable to keep other people waiting, which,
49 once for all, is a selfish and intolerable habit. But don't you hear the servant offering you
50 sherry? I wish you would attend, for my servants have quite enough to do, and can't wait all
51 the evening while you finish that very mild story to Miss Goggles. Come, leave that decanter
52 alone. I had the wine put on the table to fill up; the servants will hand it directly, or, as we
53 are a small party, I will tell you to help yourself; but, pray, do not be so officious. (There, I
54 have sent him some turbot to keep him quiet. I declare he cannot make up his mind.) You
55 are keeping my servant again, sir. Will you, or will you not, do turbot? Don't examine it in
56 that way; it is quite fresh, I assure you; take or decline it. Ah, you take it, but that is no
57 reason why you should take up a knife too. Fish, I repeat must never be touched with a
58 knife. Take a fork in the right and a small piece of bread in the left hand. Good, but—? Oh!
59 that is atrocious; of course you must not swallow the bones, but you should rather do so
60 than spit them out in that way. Put up your napkin like this, and land the said bone on your
61 plate. Don't rub your head in the sauce, my good man, nor go progging about after the
62 shrimps or oysters therein. Oh! how horrid! I declare your mouth was wide open and full of
63 fish. Small pieces, I beseech you; and once for all, whatever you eat, keep your mouth **shut**,
64 and never attempt to talk with it full.

1. Epicure in line 9 most closely means:

   a. Oaf
   b. Gourmet
   c. Gentleman
   d. Knave

2. The author's tone is:

   a. Friendly
   b. Informative
   c. Scolding
   d. Angry
   e.

3. The author incorporates which of these rhetorical elements into this text?

   a. Anecdote
   b. Comparison
   c. Alliteration
   d. Epistolary

4. Which of the following is an example of figurative language?

   a. There, I have sent him some turbot to keep him quiet.
   b. You may be sure that I never sit down to a meal without napkins.
   c. Thus an epicure will eat even macaroni with his fingers; and as sucking asparagus is more pleasant than chewing it, you may, as an epicure, take it up au naturel.
   d. It is louder than a dog lapping water, and a cat would be quite genteel to it.

5. How should fish be eaten?

   a. With a knife and fork
   b. With the fingers
   c. With a fork and piece of bread
   d. With a knife, fork and bread

6. Which of the following is an analogy?

    a. Well, but there is no occasion to throw your head back like that, you look like an alderman, sir, after dinner.

    b. I wish you would attend, for my servants have quite enough to do, and can't wait all the evening while you finish that very mild story to Miss Goggles.

    c. . So talk away to the lady on your right, and wait till soup is handed to you.

    d. But both these things are generally eaten with a fork. Bread is, of course, eaten with the fingers, and it would be absurd to carve it with your knife and fork.

7. In line 63, beseech most nearly means:

    a. Tell

    b. Beg

    c. Allow

    d. Condemn

8. The author's intention in this piece is to:

    a. Entertain

    b. Persuade

    c. Argue

    d. Teach

    e.

9. This piece can be primarily identified as:

    a. An argumentative essay

    b. A descriptive essay

    c. A narrative essay

    d. A persuasive essay

10. Which of these may you eat with your fingers?

    a. Fish

    b. Fruit

    c. Green beans

    d. Meat

1 Most of the luxuries, and many of the so-called comforts of life, are not only not
2 indispensable, but positive hindrances to the elevation of mankind. With respect to luxuries
3 and comforts, the wisest have ever lived a more simple and meagre life than the poor. The
4 ancient philosophers, Chinese, Hindoo, Persian, and Greek, were a class than which none
5 has been poorer in outward riches, none so rich in inward. We know not much about them.
6 It is remarkable that we know so much of them as we do. The same is true of the more
7 modern reformers and benefactors of their race. None can be an impartial or wise observer
8 of human life but from the vantage ground of what we should call voluntary poverty. Of a
9 life of luxury the fruit is luxury, whether in agriculture, or commerce, or literature, or art.
10 There are nowadays professors of philosophy, but not philosophers. Yet it is admirable to
11 profess because it was once admirable to live. To be a philosopher is not merely to have
12 subtle thoughts, nor even to found a school, but so to love wisdom as to live according to its
13 dictates, a life of simplicity, independence, magnanimity, and trust. It is to solve some of the
14 problems of life, not only theoretically, but practically. The success of great scholars and
15 thinkers is commonly a courtier-like success, not kingly, not manly. They make shift to live
16 merely by conformity, practically as their fathers did, and are in no sense the progenitors of
17 a noble race of men. But why do men degenerate ever? What makes families run out? What
18 is the nature of the luxury which enervates and destroys nations? Are we sure that there is
19 none of it in our own lives? The philosopher is in advance of his age even in the outward
20 form of his life. He is not fed, sheltered, clothed, warmed, like his contemporaries. How can
21 a man be a philosopher and not maintain his vital heat by better methods than other men?

22 When a man is warmed by the several modes which I have described, what does he want
23 next? Surely not more warmth of the same kind, as more and richer food, larger and more
24 splendid houses, finer and more abundant clothing, more numerous, incessant, and hotter
25 fires, and the like. When he has obtained those things which are necessary to life, there is
26 another alternative than to obtain the superfluities; and that is, to adventure on life now,
27 his vacation from humbler toil having commenced. The soil, it appears, is suited to the seed,
28 for it has sent its radicle downward, and it may now send its shoot upward also with
29 confidence. Why has man rooted himself thus firmly in the earth, but that he may rise in the
30 same proportion into the heavens above?—for the nobler plants are valued for the fruit
31 they bear at last in the air and light, far from the ground, and are not treated like the
32 humbler esculents, which, though they may be biennials, are cultivated only till they have
33 perfected their root, and often cut down at top for this purpose, so that most would not
34 know them in their flowering season.

35   I do not mean to prescribe rules to strong and valiant natures, who will mind their own
36   affairs whether in heaven or hell, and perchance build more magnificently and spend more
37   lavishly than the richest, without ever impoverishing themselves, not knowing how they
38   live—if, indeed, there are any such, as has been dreamed; nor to those who find their
39   encouragement and inspiration in precisely the present condition of things, and cherish it
40   with the fondness and enthusiasm of lovers—and, to some extent, I reckon myself in this
41   number; I do not speak to those who are well employed, in whatever circumstances, and
42   they know whether they are well employed or not;—but mainly to the mass of men who
43   are discontented, and idly complaining of the hardness of their lot or of the times, when
44   they might improve them. There are some who complain most energetically and
45   inconsolably of any, because they are, as they say, doing their duty. I also have in my mind
46   that seemingly wealthy, but most terribly impoverished class of all, who have accumulated
47   dross, but know not how to use it, or get rid of it, and thus have forged their own golden or
48   silver fetters.

11. In line 47, dross most closely means:
   a. Debt
   b. Wealth
   c. Enemies
   d. Power
   e.

12. In line 13, magnanimity most closely means:
   a. Generosity
   b. Kindness
   c. Friendliness
   d. Morality

13. Why has man rooted himself thus firmly in the earth, but that he may rise in the same proportion into the heavens above? Is an example of what rhetorical device?
   a. Chiasmus
   b. Formal language
   c. Parallelism
   d. Figurative language

14. What is the main idea of this passage?
   a. Wealth will come through hard work.
   b. Hard work is its own reward.
   c. Simplicity produces a better life.
   d. Luxuries are bad.

15. Who is the intended audience of this passage?
   a. Scholars and philosophers
   b. The nouveau riche
   c. The discontent
   d. The poor

16. "Their flowering season" in line 34 refers to:
   a. Wealth
   b. Happiness and enthusiasm
   c. Adulthood
   d. Social status
   e.

17. The author contrasts what two things?
   a. Wealth and work
   b. Voluntary poverty and luxury
   c. Work and leisure
   d. Wealth and poverty

18. The author compares wealth to:
   a. Plants
   b. Dross
   c. Fetters
   d. Monks

19. With which of the following would the author agree?
   a. Wealth is necessary for happiness.
   b. Simplicity is essential for true happiness.
   c. A comfortable life is a good thing.
   d. Hard work is its own reward.

20. This is an example of a:
   a. Narrative Essay
   b. Persuasive Essay
   c. Expository Essay
   d. Argumentative Essay

1   The statistics may be found to possess interest in several particulars. Two days in every
2   week are devoted to dueling. The rule is rigid that there must be three duels on each of
3   these days; there are generally more, but there cannot be fewer. There were six the day I
4   was present; sometimes there are seven or eight. It is insisted that eight duels a week—four
5   for each of the two days—is too low an average to draw a calculation from, but I will reckon
6   from that basis, preferring an understatement to an overstatement of the case. This
7   requires about four hundred and eighty or five hundred duelists a year—for in summer the
8   college term is about three and a half months, and in winter it is four months and
9   sometimes longer. Of the seven hundred and fifty students in the university at the time I am
10   writing of, only eighty belonged to the five corps, and it is only these corps that do the
11   dueling; occasionally other students borrow the arms and battleground of the five corps in
12   order to settle a quarrel, but this does not happen every dueling-day. [2] Consequently
13   eighty youths furnish the material for some two hundred and fifty duels a year. This average
14   gives six fights a year to each of the eighty. This large work could not be accomplished if the
15   badge-holders stood upon their privilege and ceased to volunteer.

16   They have to borrow the arms because they could not get them elsewhere or otherwise. As
17   I understand it, the public authorities, all over Germany, allow the five Corps to keep
18   swords, but do not allow them to use them. This is law is rigid; it is only the execution of it
19   that is lax.

20   Of course, where there is so much fighting, the students make it a point to keep themselves
21   in constant practice with the foil. One often sees them, at the tables in the Castle grounds,
22   using their whips or canes to illustrate some new sword trick which they have heard about;
23   and between the duels, on the day whose history I have been writing, the swords were not
24   always idle; every now and then we heard a succession of the keen hissing sounds which
25   the sword makes when it is being put through its paces in the air, and this informed us that
26   a student was practicing. Necessarily, this unceasing attention to the art develops an expert
27   occasionally. He becomes famous in his own university, his renown spreads to other
28   universities. He is invited to Goettingen, to fight with a Goettingen expert; if he is victorious,
29   he will be invited to other colleges, or those colleges will send their experts to him.
30   Americans and Englishmen often join one or another of the five corps. A year or two ago,
31   the principal Heidelberg expert was a big Kentuckian; he was invited to the various
32   universities and left a wake of victory behind him all about Germany; but at last a little
33   student in Strasburg defeated him. There was formerly a student in Heidelberg who had
34   picked up somewhere and mastered a peculiar trick of cutting up under instead of cleaving
35   down from above. While the trick lasted he won in sixteen successive duels in his university;

36 but by that time observers had discovered what his charm was, and how to break it,
37 therefore his championship ceased.

38 A rule which forbids social intercourse between members of different corps is strict. In the
39 dueling-house, in the parks, on the street, and anywhere and everywhere that the students
40 go, caps of a color group themselves together. If all the tables in a public garden were
41 crowded but one, and that one had two red-cap students at it and ten vacant places, the
42 yellow-caps, the blue-caps, the white caps, and the green caps, seeking seats, would go by
43 that table and not seem to see it, nor seem to be aware that there was such a table in the
44 grounds. The student by whose courtesy we had been enabled to visit the dueling-place,
45 wore the white cap—Prussian Corps. He introduced us to many white caps, but to none of
46 another color. The corps etiquette extended even to us, who were strangers, and required
47 us to group with the white corps only, and speak only with the white corps, while we were
48 their guests, and keep aloof from the caps of the other colors. Once I wished to examine
49 some of the swords, but an American student said, "It would not be quite polite; these now
50 in the windows all have red hilts or blue; they will bring in some with white hilts presently,
51 and those you can handle freely." When a sword was broken in the first duel, I wanted a
52 piece of it; but its hilt was the wrong color, so it was considered best and politest to await a
53 properer season.

54

21. Which corps wore the white cap?
    a. The Prussian Corps
    b. The Strasburg Corps
    c. The Heidelberg Corps
    d. The Goettingen Corps

22. What do students use to practice?
    a. Whips
    b. Canes
    c. Whips, canes or swords
    d. Whips or canes

23. Cleaving in line 34 most closely means:
    a. Splitting
    b. Stabbing
    c. Hitting
    d. Cutting

24. Where is this university and dueling field?
    a. America
    b. Canada
    c. Germany
    d. England

25. The author incorporates which of these literary tools into this passage?
    a. Anecdote
    b. Oxymoron
    c. Metaphor
    d. Allegory

26. The author's estimates of total numbers of duels and individuals involved are derived through:
    a. Exposition
    b. Inductive reasoning
    c. Deductive reasoning
    d. Logos

27. In line 46, etiquette most nearly means:
    a. Rules
    b. Manners
    c. Politeness
    d. Class

28. Line 17 is an example of:
    a. Formal language
    b. Annotation
    c. Ethos
    d. Appeal to authority

1   In the tenth year of the reign of Nero, the capital of the empire was afflicted by a fire which

2   raged beyond the memory or example of former ages. The monuments of Grecian art and

3   of Roman virtue, the trophies of the Punic and Gallic wars, the most holy temples, and the

4   most splendid palaces, were involved in one common destruction. Of the fourteen regions

5   or quarters into which Rome was divided, four only subsisted entire, three were levelled

6   with the ground, and the remaining seven, which had experienced the fury of the flames,

7   displayed a melancholy prospect of ruin and desolation. The vigilance of government

8   appears not to have neglected any of the precautions which might alleviate the sense of so

9   dreadful a calamity. The Imperial gardens were thrown open to the distressed multitude,

10   temporary buildings were erected for their accommodation, and a plentiful supply of corn

11   and provisions was distributed at a very moderate price. The most generous policy seemed

12   to have dictated the edicts which regulated the disposition of the streets and the

13   construction of private houses; and as it usually happens, in an age of prosperity, the

14   conflagration of Rome, in the course of a few years, produced a new city, more regular and

15   more beautiful than the former. But all the prudence and humanity affected by Nero on this

16   occasion were insufficient to preserve him from the popular suspicion. Every crime might be

17   imputed to the assassin of his wife and mother; nor could the prince who prostituted his

18   person and dignity on the theatre be deemed incapable of the most extravagant folly. The

19   voice of rumor accused the emperor as the incendiary of his own capital; and as the most

20   incredible stories are the best adapted to the genius of an enraged people, it was gravely

21   reported, and firmly believed, that Nero, enjoying the calamity which he had occasioned,

22   amused himself with singing to his lyre the destruction of ancient Troy. To divert a

23   suspicion, which the power of despotism was unable to suppress, the emperor resolved to

24   substitute in his own place some fictitious criminals. "With this view," continues Tacitus, "he

25   inflicted the most exquisite tortures on those men, who, under the vulgar appellation of

26   Christians, were already branded with deserved infamy. They derived their name and origin

27   from Christ, who in the reign of Tiberius had suffered death by the sentence of the

28   procurator Pontius Pilate. For a while this dire superstition was checked; but it again burst

29   forth; and not only spread itself over Judaea, the first seat of this mischievous sect, but was

30   even introduced into Rome, the common asylum which receives and protects whatever is

31   impure, whatever is atrocious. The confessions of those who were seized discovered a great

32   multitude of their accomplices, and they were all convicted, not so much for the crime of

33   setting fire to the city, as for their hatred of human kind. They died in torments, and their

34   torments were imbittered by insult and derision. Some were nailed on crosses; others sewn

35   up in the skins of wild beasts, and exposed to the fury of dogs; others again, smeared over

36   with combustible materials, were used as torches to illuminate the darkness of the night.

37   The gardens of Nero were destined for the melancholy spectacle, which was accompanied

38   with a horse-race and honored with the presence of the emperor, who mingled with the

39   populace in the dress and attitude of a charioteer. The guilt of the Christians deserved

40   indeed the most exemplary punishment, but the public abhorrence was changed into

41   commiseration, from the opinion that those unhappy wretches were sacrificed, not so much

42   to the public welfare, as to the cruelty of a jealous tyrant." Those who survey with a curious

43   eye the revolutions of mankind, may observe, that the gardens and circus of Nero on the

44   Vatican, which were polluted with the blood of the first Christians, have been rendered still

45   more famous by the triumph and by the abuse of the persecuted religion. On the same

46   spot, a temple, which far surpasses the ancient glories of the Capitol, has been since

47   erected by the Christian Pontiffs, who, deriving their claim of universal dominion from an

48   humble fisherman of Galilee, have succeeded to the throne of the Caesars, given laws to the

49   barbarian conquerors of Rome, and extended their spiritual jurisdiction from the coast of

50   the Baltic to the shores of the Pacific Ocean.

29. Which emperor reigned at the time of the fire?
   a. Caesar
   b. Pilate
   c. Nero
   d. Caligula

30. Conflagration in line 14 means:
   a. Fire
   b. Building
   c. Celebration
   d. Crime

31. This passage is an example of a:
   a. Expository
   b. Narrative
   c. Argument
   d. Description

32. In line 19, the "voice of rumor" is an example of:
    a. Allegory
    b. Anthropomorphication
    c. Metaphor
    d. Personification

33. The author relies upon which rhetorical strategies?
    a. Pathos
    b. Logos
    c. Ethos
    d. Both Pathos and Logos

34. In line 15, "affected" most nearly means:
    a. Faked
    b. Executed
    c. Produced
    d. Changed

35. There are two different points of view in this passage. The first is the author, the second is:
    a. Nero
    b. Early Christians
    c. Tacitus
    d. Tiberius

36. Words like "extravagant," "gravely," and "splendid" are examples of:
    a. Descriptive language
    b. Figurative language
    c. Formal language
    d. Argumentative language

37. What is the main idea of the long quote at the end of the passage?
    a. Christians were responsible for the fire.
    b. Nero was responsible for the fire.
    c. Nero blamed the Christians for the fire.
    d. Rome soon converted to Christianity.

38. What is the tone of the final portion of this passage?
     a. Uplifting
     b. Condemning
     c. Objective
     d. Sarcastic

1 ENGLISH travelers and writers of the sixteenth and seventeenth centuries were quite as
2 enterprising as their Continental contemporaries in telling about the coffee bean and the
3 coffee drink. The first printed reference to coffee in English, however, appears as *chaoua* in
4 a note by a Dutchman, Paludanus, in *Linschoten's Travels*, the title of an English translation
5 from the Latin of a work first published in Holland in 1595 or 1596, the English edition
6 appearing in London in 1598. A reproduction made from a photograph of the original work,
7 with the quaint black-letter German text and the Paludanus notation in roman, is shown
8 herewith.

9 Hans Hugo (or John Huygen) Van Linschooten (1563–1611) was one of the most intrepid of
10 Dutch travelers. In his description of Japanese manners and customs we find one of the
11 earliest tea references. He says:

12 Their manner of eating and drinking is: everie man hath a table alone, without table-clothes
13 or napkins, and eateth with two pieces of wood like the men of Chino: they drinke wine of
14 Rice, wherewith they drink themselves drunke, and after their meat they use a certain
15 drinke, which is a pot with hote water, which they drinke as hote as ever they may indure,
16 whether it be Winter or Summer.

17 Just here Bernard Ten Broeke Paludanus (1550–1633), Dutch savant and author, professor
18 of philosophy at the University of Leyden, himself a traveler over the four quarters of the
19 globe, inserts his note containing the coffee reference. He says:

20 The Turks holde almost the same manner of drinking of their *Chaona*, which they make of
21 certaine fruit, which is like unto the Bakelaer, and by the Egyptians called *Bon* or *Ban*: they
22 take of this fruite one pound and a half, and roast them a little in the fire and then sieth
23 them in twenty pounds of water, till the half be consumed away: this drinke they take every
24 morning fasting in their chambers, out of an earthen pot, being verie hote, as we doe here
25 drinke *aquacomposita* in the morning: and they say that it strengtheneth and maketh them
26 warme, breaketh wind, and openeth any stopping.

27 Van Linschooten then completes his tea reference by saying:

28 The manner of dressing their meat is altogether contrarie unto other nations: the aforesaid
29 warme water is made with the powder of a certaine hearbe calledChaa, which is much
30 esteemed, and is well accounted among them.

31 The *chaa* is, of course, tea, dialect *t'eh*.

32 In 1599, "Sir" Antony (or Anthony) Sherley (1565–1630), a picturesque gentleman-
33 adventurer, the first Englishman to mention coffee drinking in the Orient, sailed from

Venice on a kind of self-appointed, informal Persian mission, to invite the shah to ally himself with the Christian princes against the Turks, and incidentally, to promote English trade interests in the East. The English government knew nothing of the arrangement, disavowed him, and forbade his return to England. However, the expedition got to Persia; and the account of the voyage thither was written by William Parry, one of the Sherley party, and was published in London in 1601. It is interesting because it contains the first printed reference to coffee in English employing the more modern form of the word. The original reference was photographed for this work in the Worth Library of the British Museum, and is reproduced herewith on page 39.

The passage is part of an account of the manners and customs of the Turks (who, Parry says, are "damned infidells") in Aleppo. It reads:

They sit at their meat (which is served to them upon the ground) as Tailers sit upon their stalls, crosse-legd; for the most part, passing the day in banqueting and carowsing, untill they surfet, drinking a certaine liquor, which they do call *Coffe*, which is made of seede much like mustard seede, which will soone intoxicate the braine like our Metheglin.

Another early English reference to coffee, wherein the word is spelled "coffa", is in Captain John Smith's book of *Travels and Adventure*, published in 1603. He says of the Turks: "Their best drink is *coffa* of a graine they call *coava*."

This is the same Captain John Smith who in 1607 became the founder of the Colony of Virginia and brought with him to America probably the earliest knowledge of the beverage given to the new Western world.

Samuel Purchas (1527–1626), an early English collector of travels, in *Purchas His Pilgrimes*, under the head of "Observations of William Finch, merchant, at Socotra" (Sokotra—an island in the Indian Ocean) in 1607, says of the Arab inhabitants:

Their best entertainment is a china dish of *Coho*, a blacke bitterish drinke, made of a berry like a bayberry, brought from Mecca, supped off hot, good for the head and stomache.[51]

Still other early and favorite English references to coffee are those to be found in the *Travels* of William Biddulph. This work was published in 1609. It is entitled *The Travels of Certayne Englishmen in Africa, Asia, etc.... Begunne in 1600 and by some of them finished—this yeere 1608*. These references are also reproduced herewith from the black-letter originals in the British Museum (see page 40).

Biddulph's description of the drink, and of the coffee-house customs of the Turks, was the first detailed account to be written by an Englishman. It also appears in *Purchas His Pilgrimes* (1625). But, to quote:

Their most common drinke is *Coffa*, which is a blacke kinde of drinke, made of a kind of Pulse like Pease, called *Coaua*; which being grownd in the Mill, and boiled in water, they drinke it as hot as they can suffer it; which they finde to agree very well with them against their crudities, and feeding on hearbs and rawe meates. Other compounded drinkes they have, called *Sherbet*, made of Water and Sugar, or Hony, with Snow therein to make it coole; for although the Countrey bee hot, yet they keepe Snow all the yeere long to coole their drinke. It is accounted a great curtesie amongst them to give unto their frends when they come to visit them, a Fin-ion or Scudella of *Coffa*, which is more holesome than toothsome, for it causeth good concoction, and driveth away drowsinesse.

Some of them will also drinke Bersh or Opium, which maketh them forget themselves, and talk idely of Castles in the Ayre, as though they saw Visions, and heard Revelations. Their *Coffa* houses are more common than Ale-houses in England; but they use not so much to sit in the houses, as on benches on both sides the streets, neere unto a Coffa house, every man with his Fin-ionful; which being smoking hot, they use to put it to their Noses & Eares, and then sup it off by leasure, being full of idle and Ale-house talke whiles they are amongst themselves drinking it; if there be any news, it is talked of there.

Among other early English references to coffee we find an interesting one by Sir George Sandys (1577–1644), the poet, who gave a start to classical scholarship in America by translating Ovid's *Metamorphoses* during his pioneer days in Virginia. In 1610 he spent a year in Turkey, Egypt, and Palestine, and records of the Turks:[52]

Although they be destitute of Taverns, yet have they their Coffa-houses, which something resemble them. There sit they chatting most of the day; and sippe of a drinke called Coffa (of the berry that it is made of) in little *China* dishes as hot as they can suffer it: blacke as soote, and tasting not much unlike it (why not that blacke broth which was in use amongst the *Lacedemonians*?) which helpeth, as they say, digestion, and procureth alacrity: many of the Coffa-men keeping beautifull boyes, who serve as stales to procure them customers.

Edward Terry (1590–1660), an English traveler, writes, under date of 1616, that many of the best people in India who are strict in their religion and drink no wine at all, "use a liquor more wholesome than pleasant, they call coffee; made by a black Seed boyld in water, which turnes it almost into the same colour, but doth very little alter the taste of the water [!], notwithstanding it is very good to help Digestion, to quicken the Spirits and to cleanse the Blood."

39. The first references to coffee in English came from:
     a. Turkish novels
     b. Dutch explorers
     c. French travelers
     d. American Colonists

40. These early authors used what rhetorical device to help their reader understand coffee?
     a. Comparison
     b. Exposition
     c. Logos
     d. Pathos

41. Coffee was considered an aid to what?
     a. Religion
     b. Digestion
     c. Sleep
     d. Strength

42. The tone of the earliest authors about coffee is:
     a. Mostly Positive
     b. Largely Negative
     c. Primarily Educational
     d. Largely Aesthetic

43. The early authors compare coffee to:
     a. Tea
     b. Wine and Beer
     c. Sherbet
     d. Berries and Seeds

44. This passage is likely part of a text intended for:
     a. Coffee growers
     b. Coffee drinkers
     c. Tea drinkers
     d. Individuals who want to ban coffee

45. Identify one misunderstanding shown in these early texts:
   a. Coffee helps alertness
   b. Coffee encourages digestion
   c. Coffee is brewed from a grain
   d. Coffee is bitter

46. The early authors are, in several cases, guilty of what rhetorical fallacy?
   a. A straw man argument
   b. A false dichotomy
   c. An argument from false authority
   d. An ad hominem argument

John F. Kennedy. Inaugural Address.

1 The world is very different now. For man holds in his mortal hands the power to abolish all
2 forms of human poverty and all forms of human life. And yet the same revolutionary beliefs
3 for which our forebears fought are still at issue around the globe--the belief that the rights
4 of man come not from the generosity of the state, but from the hand of God.

5 We dare not forget today that we are the heirs of that first revolution. Let the word go forth
6 from this time and place, to friend and foe alike, that the torch has been passed to a new
7 generation of Americans--born in this century, tempered by war, disciplined by a hard and
8 bitter peace, proud of our ancient heritage, and unwilling to witness or permit the slow
9 undoing of those human rights to which this nation has always been committed, and to
10 which we are committed today at home and around the world.

11 Let every nation know, whether it wishes us well or ill, that we shall pay any price, bear any
12 burden, meet any hardship, support any friend, oppose any foe, to assure the survival and
13 the success of liberty.

14 This much we pledge--and more.

15 To those old allies whose cultural and spiritual origins we share, we pledge the loyalty of
16 faithful friends. United there is little we cannot do in a host of cooperative ventures.
17 Divided there is little we can do--for we dare not meet a powerful challenge at odds and
18 split asunder.

19 To those new states whom we welcome to the ranks of the free, we pledge our word that
20 one form of colonial control shall not have passed away merely to be replaced by a far more
21 iron tyranny. We shall not always expect to find them supporting our view. But we shall
22 always hope to find them strongly supporting their own freedom--and to remember that, in
23 the past, those who foolishly sought power by riding the back of the tiger ended up inside.

24 To those peoples in the huts and villages of half the globe struggling to break the bonds of
25 mass misery, we pledge our best efforts to help them help themselves, for whatever period
26 is required--not because the Communists may be doing it, not because we seek their votes,
27 but because it is right. If a free society cannot help the many who are poor, it cannot save
28 the few who are rich.

29 To our sister republics south of our border, we offer a special pledge: to convert our good
30 words into good deeds, in a new alliance for progress, to assist free men and free
31 governments in casting off the chains of poverty. But this peaceful revolution of hope
32 cannot become the prey of hostile powers. Let all our neighbors know that we shall join
33 with them to oppose aggression or subversion anywhere in the Americas. And let every
34 other power know that this hemisphere intends to remain the master of its own house.

35 To that world assembly of sovereign states, the United Nations, our last best hope in an age
36 where the instruments of war have far outpaced the instruments of peace, we renew our
37 pledge of support--to prevent it from becoming merely a forum for invective, to strengthen
38 its shield of the new and the weak--and to enlarge the area in which its writ may run.

39 Finally, to those nations who would make themselves our adversary, we offer not a pledge
40 but a request: that both sides begin anew the quest for peace, before the dark powers of
41 destruction unleashed by science engulf all humanity in planned or accidental self-
42 destruction.

43 We dare not tempt them with weakness. For only when our arms are sufficient beyond
44 doubt can we be certain beyond doubt that they will never be employed.

45 But neither can two great and powerful groups of nations take comfort from our present
46 course--both sides overburdened by the cost of modern weapons, both rightly alarmed by
47 the steady spread of the deadly atom, yet both racing to alter that uncertain balance of
48 terror that stays the hand of mankind's final war.

49 So let us begin anew--remembering on both sides that civility is not a sign of weakness, and
50 sincerity is always subject to proof. Let us never negotiate out of fear, but let us never fear
51 to negotiate.

52 Let both sides explore what problems unite us instead of belaboring those problems which
53 divide us. Let both sides, for the first time, formulate serious and precise proposals for the
54 inspection and control of arms, and bring the absolute power to destroy other nations
55 under the absolute control of all nations.

56 Let both sides seek to invoke the wonders of science instead of its terrors. Together let us
57 explore the stars, conquer the deserts, eradicate disease, tap the ocean depths, and
58 encourage the arts and commerce.

59 Let both sides unite to heed, in all corners of the earth, the command of Isaiah--to "undo
60 the heavy burdens, and to let the oppressed go free."

61 And, if a beachhead of cooperation may push back the jungle of suspicion, let both sides
62 join in creating a new endeavor--not a new balance of power, but a new world of law--
63 where the strong are just and the weak secure and the peace preserved.

64 All this will not be finished in the first one hundred days. Nor will it be finished in the first
65 one thousand days, nor in the life of this administration, nor even perhaps in our lifetime on
66 this planet. But let us begin.

67 In your hands, my fellow citizens, more than mine, will rest the final success or failure of our
68 course. Since this country was founded, each generation of Americans has been summoned

69 to give testimony to its national loyalty. The graves of young Americans who answered the
70 call to service surround the globe.

71 Now the trumpet summons us again--not as a call to bear arms, though arms we need--not
72 as a call to battle, though embattled we are--but a call to bear the burden of a long twilight
73 struggle, year in and year out, "rejoicing in hope; patient in tribulation," a struggle against
74 the common enemies of man: tyranny, poverty, disease, and war itself.

75 Can we forge against these enemies a grand and global alliance, North and South, East and
76 West, that can assure a more fruitful life for all mankind? Will you join in that historic
77 effort?

78 In the long history of the world, only a few generations have been granted the role of
79 defending freedom in its hour of maximum danger. I do not shrink from this responsibility--I
80 welcome it. I do not believe that any of us would exchange places with any other people or
81 any other generation. The energy, the faith, the devotion which we bring to this endeavor
82 will light our country and all who serve it. And the glow from that fire can truly light the
83 world.

84 And so, my fellow Americans, ask not what your country can do for you--ask what you can
85 do for your country.

86 My fellow citizens of the world, ask not what America will do for you, but what together we
87 can do for the freedom of man.

88 Finally, whether you are citizens of America or citizens of the world, ask of us here the same
89 high standards of strength and sacrifice which we ask of you. With a good conscience our
90 only sure reward, with history the final judge of our deeds, let us go forth to lead the land
91 we love, asking his blessing and his help, but knowing that here on earth God's work must
92 truly be our own.
93

47. This speech relies primarily upon both:
    a. Logos and ethos
    b. Ethos and pathos
    c. Pathos and logos
    d. Ethos and logos

48. What is the overall tone of this passage?
    a. Angry
    b. Hopeful
    c. Frustrated
    d. Despondent

49. "Invective" in line 37 most nearly means:
    a. Insults
    b. War
    c. Violence
    d. Negotiations

50. "The belief that the rights of man come not from the generosity of the state, but from the hand of God," in line 4 is an example of:
    a. An appeal to authority
    b. An appeal to false authority
    c. An ad hominem argument
    d. Figurative language

51. Lines 84-85 illustrate which rhetorical tool?
    a. Asyndeton
    b. Cacophony
    c. Euphemism
    d. Hyperbole

52. Line 57 is an example of:
   a. Simile
   b. Metaphor
   c. Allegory
   d. Anecdote

53. In line 23, "those who foolishly sought power by riding the back of the tiger ended up inside," means:
   a. Riding tigers is a bad idea
   b. Attempting to overthrow democracy will result in war
   c. Young democracies are like tigers
   d. New democracies are often located in jungles with tigers

54. Lines 67 to 70 illustrate what rhetorical device?
   a. Paradox
   b. Analogy
   c. Parallelism
   d. Understatement

55. "Tribulation" in line 73 most nearly means:
   a. Happiness
   b. Peace
   c. War
   d. Struggle

From Ralph Waldo Emerson's 1841 essay on Self Reliance. Read this passage and write an essay explaining how Emerson used language and rhetoric in his writing.

I read the other day some verses written by an eminent painter which were original and not conventional. The soul always hears an admonition in such lines, let the subject be what it may. The sentiment they instill is of more value than any thought they may contain. To believe your own thought, to believe that what is true for you in your private heart is true for all men,—that is genius. Speak your latent conviction, and it shall be the universal sense; for the inmost in due time becomes the outmost,—and our first thought is rendered back to us by the trumpets of the Last Judgment. Familiar as the voice of the mind is to each, the highest merit we ascribe to Moses, Plato, and Milton is, that they set at naught books and traditions, and spoke not what men, but what they thought. A man should learn to detect and watch that gleam of light which flashes across his mind from within, more than the luster of the firmament of bards and sages. Yet he dismisses without notice his thought, because it is his. In every work of genius we recognize our own rejected thoughts: they come back to us with a certain alienated majesty. Great works of art have no more affecting lesson for us than this. They teach us to abide by our spontaneous impression with good-humored inflexibility then most when the whole cry of voices is on the other side. Else, to-morrow a stranger will say with masterly good sense precisely what we have thought and felt all the time, and we shall be forced to take with shame our own opinion from another.

There is a time in every man's education when he arrives at the conviction that envy is ignorance; that imitation is suicide; that he must take himself for better, for worse, as his portion; that though the wide universe is full of good, no kernel of nourishing corn can come to him but through his toil bestowed on that plot of ground which is given to him to till. The power which resides in him is new in nature, and none but he knows what that is which he can do, nor does he know until he has tried. Not for nothing one face, one character, one fact, makes much impression on him, and another none. This sculpture in the memory is not without preëstablished harmony. The eye was placed where one ray should fall, that it might testify of that particular ray. We but half express ourselves, and are ashamed of that divine idea which each of us represents. It may be safely trusted as proportionate and of good issues, so it be faithfully imparted, but God will not have his work made manifest by cowards. A man is relieved and gay when he has put his heart into his work and done his best; but what he has said or done otherwise shall give him no peace. It is a deliverance which does not deliver. In the attempt his genius deserts him; no muse befriends; no invention, no hope.

Trust thyself: every heart vibrates to that iron string. Accept the place the divine providence has found for you, the society of your contemporaries, the connection of events. Great men have always done so, and confided themselves childlike to the genius of their age, betraying their perception that the absolutely trustworthy was seated at their heart, working through their hands, predominating in all their being. And we are now men, and must accept in the highest mind the same transcendent destiny; and not minors and invalids in a protected corner, not cowards fleeing before a revolution, but guides, redeemers, and benefactors, obeying the Almighty effort, and advancing on Chaos and the Dark.

This short excerpt, taken from Francis Bacon's On Empire discusses rule and the state. Your argumentative essay should refute, support or qualify this text and interpretation of power and leadership.

IT IS a miserable state of mind, to have few things to desire, and many things to fear; and yet that commonly is the case of kings; who, being at the highest, want matter of desire, which makes their minds more languishing; and have many representations of perils and shadows, which makes their minds the less clear. And this is one reason also, of that effect which the Scripture speaketh of, That the king's heart is inscrutable. For multitude of jealousies, and lack of some predominant desire, that should marshal and put in order all the rest, maketh any man's heart, hard to find or sound. Hence it comes likewise, that princes many times make themselves desires, and set their hearts upon toys; sometimes upon a building; sometimes upon erecting of an order; sometimes upon the advancing of a person; sometimes upon obtaining excellency in some art, or feat of the hand; as Nero for playing on the harp, Domitian for certainty of the hand with the arrow, Commodus for playing at fence, Caracalla for driving chariots, and the like. This seemeth incredible, unto those that know not the principle, that the mind of man, is more cheered and refreshed by profiting in small things, than by standing at a stay, in great. We see also that kings that have been fortunate conquerors, in their first years, it being not possible for them to go forward infinitely, but that they must have some check, or arrest in their fortunes, turn in their latter years to be superstitious, and melancholy; as did Alexander the Great; Diocletian; and in our memory, Charles the Fifth; and others: for he that is used to go forward, and findeth a stop, falleth out of his own favor, and is not the thing he was.

To speak now of the true temper of empire, it is a thing rare and hard to keep; for both temper, and distemper, consist of contraries. But it is one thing, to mingle contraries, another to interchange them. The answer of Apollonius to Vespasian, is full of excellent instruction. Vespasian asked him, What was Nero's overthrow? He answered, Nero could touch and tune the harp well; but in government, sometimes he used to wind the pins too high, sometimes to let them down too low. And certain it is, that nothing destroyeth authority so much, as the unequal and untimely interchange of power pressed too far, and relaxed too much.

This is true, that the wisdom of all these latter times, in princes' affairs, is rather fine deliveries, and shiftings of dangers and mischiefs, when they are near, than solid and grounded courses to keep them aloof. But this is but to try masteries with fortune. And let men beware, how they neglect and suffer matter of trouble to be prepared; for no man can forbid the spark, nor tell whence it may come. The difficulties in princes' business are many and great; but the greatest difficulty, is often in their own mind. For it is common with princes (saith Tacitus) to will contradictories, Sunt plerumque regum voluntates vehementes, et inter se contrariae. For it is the solecism of power, to think to command the end, and yet not to endure the mean.

Kings have to deal with their neighbors, their wives, their children, their prelates or clergy, their nobles, their second-nobles or gentlemen, their merchants, their commons, and their men of war; and from all these arise dangers, if care and circumspection be not used.

These three sources focus on Marie Antoinette's role as a figure in the French court and pivotal figure in the beginning of the French Revolution. Bring at least two of these three sources together, synthesizing them to produce your own exposition and insights into the role and life of Marie Antoinette.

Hilare Belloc. The French Revolution. 1911.

Marie Antoinette presents to history a character which it is of the highest interest to regard as a whole. It is the business of her biographers to consider that character as a whole; but in her connection with the Revolution there is but one aspect of it which is of importance, and that is the attitude which such a character was bound to take towards the French nation in the midst of which the Queen found herself.

It is the solution of the whole problem which the Queen's action sets before us to apprehend the gulf that separated her not only from the French temperament, but from a comprehension of all French society. Had she been a woman lacking in energy or in decision, this alien character in her would have been a small matter, and her ignorance of the French in every form of their activity, or rather her inability to comprehend them, would have been but a private failing productive only of certain local and immediate consequences, and not in any way determining the great lines of the revolutionary movement.[Pg 46]

As it was, her energy was not only abundant but steadfast; it grew more secure in its action as it increased with her years, and the initiative which gave that energy its course never vacillated, but was always direct. She knew her own mind, and she attempted, often with a partial success, to realise her convictions. There was no character in touch with the Executive during the first years of the Revolution comparable to hers for fixity of purpose and definition of view.

It was due to this energy and singleness of aim that her misunderstanding of the material with which she had to deal was of such fatal importance.

It was she who chose, before the outbreak of the Revolution, the succession of those ministers both Liberal and Reactionary, whose unwise plans upon either side precipitated violence. It was she who called and then revoked, and later recalled to office the wealthy and over-estimated Necker; she who substituted for him, and then so inopportunely threw over Calonne, the most national of the precursors of the Revolution, and ever after her most bitter enemy; it was she who advised the more particularly irritating details of resistance after the meeting of the first revolutionary Parliament; it was she who presided over (and helped to warp) the plans for the flight of the royal family; it was she who, after this flight had failed, framed a definite scheme for the coercion of the French people by the

Governments of Europe; it was she who betrayed to foreign chanceries[Pg 47] the French plan of campaign when war had become inevitable; finally, it was she who inspired the declaration of Brunswick which accompanied the invasion of French territory, and she was in particular the author of the famous threat therein contained to give over Paris to military execution, and to hold all the popular authorities responsible with their lives for the restoration of the pre-revolutionary state of affairs.

As research proceeds, the capital effect of this woman's continual and decided interference will be more and more apparent to historians.

Now Marie Antoinette's conception of mankind in general was the conception that you will find prevalent in such societies as that domestic and warm centre which had nourished her childhood. The romantic affection of a few equals, the personal loyalty of a handful of personal servants, the vague histrionic content which permeates the poor at the sight of great equipages and rich accoutrements, the cheers of a crowd when such symbols accompanying monarchy are displayed in the streets—all these were for Marie Antoinette the fundamental political feelings of mankind. An absence of them she regarded with bewilderment, an active opposition to them she hated as something at once incomprehensible and positively evil.

Edmund Burke - 1793

It is now sixteen or seventeen years since I saw the Queen of France, then the Dauphiness, at Versailles; and surely never lighted on this orb, which she hardly seemed to touch, a more delightful vision. I saw her just above the horizon, decorating and cheering the elevated sphere she had just begun to move in, glittering like the morning star full of life and splendor and joy.

Oh, what a revolution! and what a heart must I have, to contemplate without emotion that elevation and that fall! Little did I dream, when she added titles of veneration to those of enthusiastic, distant, respectful love, that she should ever be obliged to carry the sharp antidote against disgrace concealed in that bosom; little did I dream that I should have lived to see such disasters fallen upon her, in a nation of gallant men, in a nation of men of honor, and of cavaliers! I thought ten thousand swords must have leaped from their scabbards, to avenge even a look that threatened her with insult.

But the age of chivalry is gone; that of sophisters, economists, and calculators has succeeded, and the glory of Europe is extinguished forever. Never, never more, shall we behold that generous loyalty to rank and sex, that proud submission, that dignified obedience, that subordination of the heart, which kept alive, even in servitude itself, the spirit of an exalted freedom! The unbought grace of life, the cheap defense of nations, the nurse of manly sentiment and heroic enterprise is gone. It is gone, that sensibility of principle, that chastity of honor, which felt a stain like a wound, which inspired courage whilst it mitigated ferocity, which ennobled whatever it touched, and under which vice itself lost half its evil, by losing all its grossness.

Mme. Campan. Memoirs of the Court of Marie Antoinette, Queen of France.

We have already seen what changes had been made in the Temple. Marie Antoinette had been separated from her sister, her daughter, and her Son, by virtue of a decree which ordered the trial and exile of the last members of the family of the Bourbons. She had been removed to the Conciergerie, and there, alone in a narrow prison, she was reduced to what was strictly necessary, like the other prisoners. The imprudence of a devoted friend had rendered her situation still more irksome. Michonnis, a member of the municipality, in whom she had excited a warm interest, was desirous of introducing to her a person who, he said, wished to see her out of curiosity. This man, a courageous emigrant, threw to her a carnation, in which was enclosed a slip of very fine paper with these words: "Your friends are ready,"—false hope, and equally dangerous for her who received it, and for him who gave it! Michonnis and the emigrant were detected and forthwith apprehended; and the vigilance exercised in regard to the unfortunate prisoner became from that day more rigorous than ever.

[The Queen was lodged in a room called the council chamber, which was considered as the moat unwholesome apartment in the Conciergerie on account of its dampness and the bad smells by which it was continually affected. Under pretence of giving her a person to wait upon her they placed near her a spy,—a man of a horrible countenance and hollow, sepulchral voice. This wretch, whose name was Barassin, was a robber and murderer by profession. Such was the chosen attendant on the Queen of France! A few days before her trial this wretch was removed and a gendarme placed in her chamber, who watched over her night and day, and from whom she was not separated, even when in bed, but by a ragged curtain. In this melancholy abode Marie Antoinette had no other dress than an old black gown, stockings with holes, which she was forced to mend every day; and she was entirely destitute of shoes.—DU BROCA.]

Gendarmes were to mount guard incessantly at the door of her prison, and they were expressly forbidden to answer anything that she might say to them.

That wretch Hebert, the deputy of Chaumette, and editor of the disgusting paper Pere Duchesne, a writer of the party of which Vincent, Ronsin, Varlet, and Leclerc were the leaders—Hebert had made it his particular business to torment the unfortunate remnant of the dethroned family. He asserted that the family of the tyrant ought not to be better treated than any sans-culotte family; and he had caused a resolution to be passed by which the sort of luxury in which the prisoners in the Temple were maintained was to be suppressed. They were no longer to be allowed either poultry or pastry; they were reduced to one sort of aliment for breakfast, and to soup or broth and a single dish for dinner, to two dishes for supper, and half a bottle of wine apiece. Tallow candles were to be furnished instead of wag, pewter instead of silver plate, and delft ware instead of porcelain. The wood and water carriers alone were permitted to enter their room, and that only accompanied by two commissioners. Their food was to be introduced to them by means of a turning box. The numerous establishment was reduced to a cook and an assistant, two men-servants, and a woman-servant to attend to the linen.

As soon as this resolution was passed, Hebert had repaired to the Temple and inhumanly taken away from the unfortunate prisoners even the most trifling articles to which they attached a high value. Eighty Louis which Madame Elisabeth had in reserve, and which she had received from Madame de Lamballe, were also taken away. No one is more dangerous, more cruel, than the man without acquirements, without education, clothed with a recent authority. If, above all, he possess a base nature, if, like Hebert, who was check-taker at the door of a theatre, and embezzled money out of the receipts, he be destitute of natural morality, and if he leap all at once from the mud of his condition into power, he is as mean as he is atrocious. Such was Hebert in his conduct at the Temple. He did not confine himself to the annoyances which we have mentioned. He and some others conceived the idea of separating the young Prince from his aunt and sister. A shoemaker named Simon and his wife were the instructors to whom it was deemed right to consign him for the purpose of giving him a sans-cullotte education. Simon and his wife were shut up in the Temple, and, becoming prisoners with the unfortunate child, were directed to bring him up in their own way. Their food was better than that of the Princesses, and they shared the table of the municipal commissioners who were on duty. Simon was permitted to go down, accompanied by two commissioners, to the court of the Temple, for the purpose of giving the Dauphin a little exercise.

Hebert conceived the infamous idea of wringing from this boy revelations to criminate his unhappy mother. Whether this wretch imputed to the child false revelations, or abused his, tender age and his condition to extort from him what admissions soever he pleased, he obtained a revolting deposition; and as the youth of the Prince did not admit of his being brought before the tribunal, Hebert appeared and detailed the infamous particulars which he had himself either dictated or invented.

Answer Key Practice Test 1

1. b	2. c	3. a	4. d	5. c	6. a	7. b
8. d	9. d	10. b	11. b	12. a	13. d	14. c
15. c	16. b	17. a	18. c	19. b	20. b	21. a
22. c	23. c	24. c	25. a	26. b	27. a	28. b
29. c	30. a	31. b	32. d	33. b	34. c	35. c
36. a	37. c	38. b	39. b	40. a	41. b	42. b
43. d	44. a	45. c	46. a	47. b	48. b	49. a
50. a	51. a	52. b	53. b	54. c	55. d	

Expository Essay

Ralph Waldo Emerson's "Self-Reliance" is an exercise in allusion and aphorisms, reference and repetition. This passage is only a portion of the whole, but reveals Emerson's skill with language, particularly figurative language, and rhetoric. He relies upon traditional techniques to make a very non-traditional point. Rather than emphasizing the value of education, learning and tradition, Emerson emphatically supports the notion of self-reliance, of self-determination, and of sudden and even emotional insights.

While Emerson writes specifically about self-reliance, he begins his essay by making allusions to well-known authors and sources. He first references a quote or epigraph from an unnamed artist, but goes on to allude to well-known thinkers, including Moses, in the Old Testament, the Greek philosopher Plato, and the writer John Milton. While all three of these could be considered teachers or writers, he emphasizes their independence and self-reliance. They are all, first and foremost, thinkers. They did not rely on the works of others, but on their own thoughts. They are alluded to not as justification or authority, but as an example for others. They did not repeat what they learned, but made their own leaps of logic, providing others with new directions.

Moses, Milton and Plato are not Emerson's only examples of self-reliance. He creates his own examples, incorporating aspects of traditional sayings or aphorisms, like "trust thyself" in his text. He relies upon some traditional examples, referring, for instance to "divine providence" to add authority to his argument. In this, his use of tradition supports a relatively non-traditional ideal. Self-reliance is fundamentally contrary to many of the ideas associated with tradition, from religion to education, but Emerson uses the ethos or respectability of these sources in defense of his argument.

Emerson's Self-Reliance may be called a persuasive essay, but it is also an example of skillful prose, rich with figurative language and imagery. He compares the work of learning and thinking to the physical labor of working the soil to produce food; however, in this case, the food is thought. He stresses the importance of the individual, whether he responds to another person, a work of art or anything else. The individual is identified as "that divine idea which each of us represents". Again, Emerson relies upon divine authority to persuade the reader of something that moves beyond traditional doctrines of free will and into a new independence.

While the thesis of this essay may be simple, stating the importance of independent thought, the text itself is complex. Emerson relies upon a variety of sources and authorities to create a text that suggests that the reader disregard outside authority. In this, Emerson's text presents a rhetorical paradox. We are to believe in the authority of the author and his sources, as they tell us not to believe in anything but ourselves.

Argumentative Essay

With great power comes great responsibility. This very modern statement reflects the essential thesis of Francis Bacon's "On Empire." Bacon identifies, in his essay, the very real challenges of government, both on a personal and a political scale. While his discussion of empire focuses on monarchy, it is applicable to monarchial governments of the past, modern government and even modern business empires. In all of these cases, the powerful may want for nothing, but have little of true value.

Bacon begins "On Empire" by discussing the very real dilemma at the heart of life for a king. He has all that he can want, but fears nearly everything. In this, "want matter of desire" refers not to friends, compatriots or relationships, but material goods. The king thus fears, not for his material well-being, but for the relationships in his life. He is at risk of treachery from all those around him, like the business tycoon of today who trusts no one on his own board of directors.

This very frame of existence, this "miserable state of mind" affects every aspect of life for the most powerful of individuals. Eventually, according to Bacon, the result is the demise of the wealthy. He cites Nero's madness and the fall of Alexander the Great, alluding to the drawbacks of power, particularly power gained at a young age. The individual who gains power young may not have the ability to handle adversity, leading to failure as great as his success. Today, we see the same in young celebrities, reaching the height of their fame as teens, and falling progressively as young adults. Power and fame provides no security, no safety, and now, as then, leaves the individual fearful and wanting that which, because of fame and power, they cannot have.

Bacon identifies the greatest difficulty for the ruler as that within his own mind. He is less at risk from those around him than he is his own fears and weaknesses. This too, remains true even today. The ruler or individual who is able to continue to act thoughtfully and to lead well has little to fear. He will be respected, and can establish relationships. Failing to act thoughtfully and lead well opens the leader up to the potential machinations of those around him, seeking their own power. He becomes less feared and more hated, eventually leading to his own downfall. It becomes clear that not all can handle the responsibility that comes with power.

Bacon's On Empire may be a dated essay, referencing figures from the ancient past, but the wisdom shared in this piece remains relevant for the wealthy, the successful and the powerful. All of the goods and wealth will provide no satisfaction when faced with fear and worry. Eventually that very fear and worry will lead to a great failure and fall from a place of glory.

Synthesis Essay

Marie Antoinette has entered the modern imagination as a character, but she was a woman, a queen and a mother. History has painted her as an adulterous villainess, a scheming witch, and a queen willing to watch her people starve while she played in a pretty palace. These three pieces, including two from the 18th century, present very different views of Marie Antoinette, as a young princess, a queen and a prisoner.

Edmund Burke describes the queen as a young woman, still the dauphiness, or crown princess, of France. She was "glittering like the morning star of light." Burke's description suggests beauty, a princess putting forth the image she had been raised to show. Presumably not yet a mother, she was young, beautiful, and served as the highest-ranking female in the court. The historical text focuses on Marie Antoinette as queen. In this, she is not glittering or presenting a divine vision. Instead, she seems petty, selfish, and unable to relate to reality. Finally, one of her contemporaries, her own ladies, told the story of her fall. Marie Antoinette was no longer queen. She had been a prisoner for years, had lost her children and husband and was on trial for her life. Her story is a sad one, but it is a concrete one, told as Campan saw it. As history tells us, she would be condemned to die. These three sources, together, form a chronology of Marie Antoinette's life.

While these three pieces share the same subject and two of the three were written not long after Marie Antoinette's own lifetime, they each have a very different tone. Burke reminisces about a glimpse of a young princess. He did not know her, but was astounded by the image she presented. Here, Marie Antoinette stands as an image of the French court before its fall. For Madame Campan, this was the story of a woman she knew deeply and personally, as she served as a lady-in-waiting to her. While she writes with relatively little emotion, she is, nonetheless, sympathetic to the queen. The historian is not bowled over by the queen, nor does he have a personal relationship. He is also the most negative of the three, presenting her as a factor in the eventual French Revolution, bloody as it was. Here, the personal impact of an individual on a narrative becomes clear. Even if history did not favor the queen, both Burke and Campan were kinder to her. She was, for them, an individual, rather than simply a historical figure.

Just as the tone differs, the purpose of each of these differs. Burke's speech is expository, relying upon figurative language to share the experience of seeing the dauphiness. Campan's work is narrative, sharing the story as she witnessed it. Finally, the historian, Belloc, writes an educational piece. His intent is to inform, but this too, is colored by his time. For Belloc, Marie Antoinette held power and abused that power.

Historians have a number of sources available to them, including contemporary documents. Belloc likely read Campan's story of her own experiences with Marie Antoinette and was aware of experiences like Burke's. While he must have known of these, he made a villain of the queen. His discussion is not an objective one, but a subjective one. In these three pieces, we see the rise of the princess, the power of the queen, and the fall of a sick and dying woman.

Practice Test 2

John Dewey. Democracy and Education.

1   The Social Environment. A being whose activities are associated with others has a social
2   environment. What he does and what he can do depend upon the expectations, demands,
3   approvals, and condemnations of others. A being connected with other beings cannot
4   perform his own activities without taking the activities of others into account. For they are
5   the indispensable conditions of the realization of his tendencies. When he moves he stirs
6   them and reciprocally. We might as well try to imagine a business man doing business,
7   buying and selling, all by himself, as to conceive it possible to define the activities of an
8   individual in terms of his isolated actions. The manufacturer moreover is as truly socially
9   guided in his activities when he is laying plans in the privacy of his own counting house as
10 when he is buying his raw material or selling his finished goods. Thinking and feeling that
11 have to do with action in association with others is as much a social mode of behavior as is
12 the most overt cooperative or hostile act.

13 What we have more especially to indicate is how the social medium nurtures its immature
14 members. There is no great difficulty in seeing how it shapes the external habits of action.
15 Even dogs and horses have their actions modified by association with human beings; they
16 form different habits because human beings are concerned with what they do. Human
17 beings control animals by controlling the natural stimuli which influence them; by creating a
18 certain environment in other words. Food, bits and bridles, noises, vehicles, are used to
19 direct the ways in which the natural or instinctive responses of horses occur. By operating
20 steadily to call out certain acts, habits are formed which function with the same uniformity
21 as the original stimuli. If a rat is put in a maze and finds food only by making a given number
22 of turns in a given sequence, his activity is gradually modified till he habitually takes that
23 course rather than another when he is hungry.

24 Human actions are modified in a like fashion. A burnt child dreads the fire; if a parent
25 arranged conditions so that every time a child touched a certain toy he got burned, the child
26 would learn to avoid that toy as automatically as he avoids touching fire. So far, however,
27 we are dealing with what may be called training in distinction from educative teaching. The
28 changes considered are in outer action rather than in mental and emotional dispositions of
29 behavior. The distinction is not, however, a sharp one. The child might conceivably generate
30 in time a violent antipathy, not only to that particular toy, but to the class of toys
31 resembling it. The aversion might even persist after he had forgotten about the original
32 burns; later on he might even invent some reason to account for his seemingly irrational

antipathy. In some cases, altering the external habit of action by changing the environment to affect the stimuli to action will also alter the mental disposition concerned in the action. Yet this does not always happen; a person trained to dodge a threatening blow, dodges automatically with no corresponding thought or emotion. We have to find, then, some differentia of training from education.

A clew may be found in the fact that the horse does not really share in the social use to which his action is put. Some one else uses the horse to secure a result which is advantageous by making it advantageous to the horse to perform the act—he gets food, etc. But the horse, presumably, does not get any new interest. He remains interested in food, not in the service he is rendering. He is not a partner in a shared activity. Were he to become a copartner, he would, in engaging in the conjoint activity, have the same interest in its accomplishment which others have. He would share their ideas and emotions.

Now in many cases—too many cases—the activity of the immature human being is simply played upon to secure habits which are useful. He is trained like an animal rather than educated like a human being. His instincts remain attached to their original objects of pain or pleasure. But to get happiness or to avoid the pain of failure he has to act in a way agreeable to others. In other cases, he really shares or participates in the common activity. In this case, his original impulse is modified. He not merely acts in a way agreeing with the actions of others, but, in so acting, the same ideas and emotions are aroused in him that animate the others. A tribe, let us say, is warlike. The successes for which it strives, the achievements upon which it sets store, are connected with fighting and victory. The presence of this medium incites bellicose exhibitions in a boy, first in games, then in fact when he is strong enough. As he fights he wins approval and advancement; as he refrains, he is disliked, ridiculed, shut out from favorable recognition. It is not surprising that his original belligerent tendencies and emotions are strengthened at the expense of others, and that his ideas turn to things connected with war. Only in this way can he become fully a recognized member of his group. Thus his mental habitudes are gradually assimilated to those   of   his   group.

1. "Food, bits and bridles, noises, vehicles, are used to direct the ways in which the natural or instinctive responses of horses occur," in lines 18-21 shows the use of:
    a. Illustrative examples
    b. Metaphor
    c. Simile
    d. Analogy

2. "Belligerent" in line 57 most nearly means:
    a. Aggressive
    b. Submissive
    c. Peaceful
    d. Angry

3. The horse is referenced as:
    a. An example of training
    b. An example of education
    c. An example of social behavior
    d. An example of social compliance

4. In lines 46 and 47, "He is trained like an animal rather than educated like a human being," is an example of what:
    a. Metaphor
    b. Simile
    c. Allegory
    d. Pathos

5. Which of the following represents the use of an anecdote?
    a. We might as well try to imagine a business man doing business, buying and selling, all by himself, as to conceive it possible to define the activities of an individual in terms of his isolated actions.
    b. A burnt child dreads the fire; if a parent arranged conditions so that every time a child touched a certain toy he got burned, the child would learn to avoid that toy as automatically as he avoids touching fire.
    c. Some one else uses the horse to secure a result which is advantageous by making it advantageous to the horse to perform the act—he gets food, etc.
    d. Only in this way can he become fully a recognized member of his group. Thus his mental habitudes are gradually assimilated to those of his group.

6. The author favors:
    a. Concrete language
    b. Abstract language
    c. Figurative language
    d. Colloquial language

7. This passage is an example of:
    a. A narrative essay
    b. An expository essay
    c. An argumentative essay
    d. A persuasive essay

8. What is the main idea of this passage?
    a. Humans are educated.
    b. Humans are trained.
    c. Animals are trained.
    d. Social behavior is learned.

9. The author's tone is:
    a. Angry
    b. Lighthearted
    c. Educational
    d. Morose

10. This passage relies upon:
   a. Comparison and contrasts
   b. Connotations
   c. Appeals to authority
   d. Appeals to emotion

11. In line 59, "assimilated" most nearly means:
   a. Compared
   b. Likened
   c. Misconstrued
   d. Referred

12. Based on the author's point of view, with which of the following statements would he agree?
   a. Human thought and behavior is based on social contacts and interactions.
   b. Human thought and personality is present at birth.
   c. Animals and humans learn in the same way.
   d. Children should be trained to behave appropriately.

Susan B. Anthony , 1873

1   Friends and fellow citizens: I stand before you tonight under indictment for the alleged
2   crime of having voted at the last presidential election, without having a lawful right to vote.
3   It shall be my work this evening to prove to you that in thus voting, I not only committed no
4   crime, but, instead, simply exercised my citizen's rights, guaranteed to me and all United
5   States citizens by the National Constitution, beyond the power of any state to deny.

6   The preamble of the Federal Constitution says:

7   "We, the people of the United States, in order to form a more perfect union, establish
8   justice, insure domestic tranquility, provide for the common defense, promote the general
9   welfare, and secure the blessings of liberty to ourselves and our posterity, do ordain and
10 establish this Constitution for the United States of America."

11 It was we, the people; not we, the white male citizens; nor yet we, the male citizens; but
12 we, the whole people, who formed the Union. And we formed it, not to give the blessings of
13 liberty, but to secure them; not to the half of ourselves and the half of our posterity, but to
14 the whole people - women as well as men. And it is a downright mockery to talk to women
15 of their enjoyment of the blessings of liberty while they are denied the use of the only
16 means of securing them provided by this democratic-republican government - the ballot.

17 For any state to make sex a qualification that must ever result in the disfranchisement of
18 one entire half of the people, is to pass a bill of attainder, or, an ex post facto law, and is
19 therefore a violation of the supreme law of the land. By it the blessings of liberty are forever
20 withheld from women and their female posterity.

21 To them this government has no just powers derived from the consent of the governed. To
22 them this government is not a democracy. It is not a republic. It is an odious aristocracy; a
23 hateful oligarchy of sex; the most hateful aristocracy ever established on the face of the
24 globe; an oligarchy of wealth, where the rich govern the poor. An oligarchy of learning,
25 where the educated govern the ignorant, or even an oligarchy of race, where the Saxon
26 rules the African, might be endured; but this oligarchy of sex, which makes father, brothers,
27 husband, sons, the oligarchs over the mother and sisters, the wife and daughters, of every
28 household - which ordains all men sovereigns, all women subjects, carries dissension,
29 discord, and rebellion into every home of the nation.

30 Webster, Worcester, and Bouvier all define a citizen to be a person in the United States,
31 entitled to vote and hold office.

32 The only question left to be settled now is: Are women persons? And I hardly believe any of
33 our opponents will have the hardihood to say they are not. Being persons, then, women are
34 citizens; and no state has a right to make any law, or to enforce any old law, that shall

35 abridge their privileges or immunities. Hence, every discrimination against women in the
36 constitutions and laws of the several states is today null and void, precisely as is every one
37 against Negroes.

38 Susan B. Anthony - 1873

13. In lines 30p and 31, "a citizen to be a person in the United States, entitled to vote and hold office" is an example of:
   a. Figurative language
   b. Denotation
   c. Connotation
   d. Colloquialism

14. The repetition found in the paragraph in lines 23-29 is an example of:
   a. Analogy
   b. Anachronism
   c. Anaphora
   d. Anadiplosis

15. An oligarchy in lines 23 and onward is best defined as:
   a. A democratic form of government
   b. A royal form of government
   c. A government led by a tyrant
   d. A government led by only a few

16. "It was we, the people; not we, the white male citizens; nor yet we, the male citizens; but we, the whole people, who formed the Union." In lines 11 and 12 illustrates the use of:
   a. Parallelism
   b. Pathos
   c. Paradox
   d. Persuasion

17. The author's purpose in writing this passage was to:
    a. Convince the reader to support women's suffrage
    b. Convince the reader to support civil rights
    c. Convince the reader to support the rights of the poor
    d. Convince the reader to oppose civil rights

18. Disenfranchisement most nearly means:
    a. Voting rights
    b. Loss of voting rights
    c. Loss of civil rights
    d. Civil rights

19. The author compares a lack of voting rights for women to a lack of voting rights for:
    a. Men
    b. African-Americans
    c. The uneducated
    d. White men

20. Anthony's argument is based on:
    a. An appeal to false authority
    b. An appeal to the authority of the Constitution
    c. An appeal to the authority of the government
    d. An appeal to the authority of the church

21. This passage was likely originally a:
    a. Newspaper editorial
    b. Article in a magazine
    c. Speech
    d. Part of a book

22. In line 33, "hardihood" most nearly means:
    a. Strength
    b. Weakness
    c. Poor judgment
    d. Foolishness

23. Anthony relies on:
    a. Ethos
    b. Pathos
    c. Logos
    d. None of the above

Frederick Douglass. Narrative of the Life of an American Slave.

1   I did not, when a slave, understand the deep meaning of those rude and apparently

2   incoherent songs. I was myself within the circle; so that I neither saw nor heard as those

3   without might see and hear. They told a tale of woe which was then altogether beyond my

4   feeble comprehension; they were tones loud, long, and deep; they breathed the prayer and

5   complaint of souls boiling over with the bitterest anguish. Every tone was a testimony

6   against slavery, and a prayer to God for deliverance from chains. The hearing of those wild

7   notes always depressed my spirit, and filled me with ineffable sadness. I have frequently

8   found myself in tears while hearing them. The mere recurrence to those songs, even now,

9   afflicts me; and while I am writing these lines, an expression of feeling has already found its

10   way down my cheek. To those songs I trace my first glimmering conception of the

11   dehumanizing character of slavery. I can never get rid of that conception. Those songs still

12   follow me, to deepen my hatred of slavery, and quicken my sympathies for my brethren in

13   bonds. If any one wishes to be impressed with the soul-killing effects of slavery, let him go

14   to Colonel Lloyd's plantation, and, on allowance-day, place himself in the deep pine woods,

15   and there let him, in silence, analyze the sounds that shall pass through the chambers of his

16   soul,—and if he is not thus impressed, it will only be because "there is no flesh in his

17   obdurate heart."

18   I have often been utterly astonished, since I came to the north, to find persons who could

19   speak of the singing, among slaves, as evidence of their contentment and happiness. It is

20   impossible to conceive of a greater mistake. Slaves sing most when they are most unhappy.

21   The songs of the slave represent the sorrows of his heart; and he is relieved by them, only

22   as an aching heart is relieved by its tears. At least, such is my experience. I have often sung

23   to drown my sorrow, but seldom to express my happiness. Crying for joy, and singing for

24   joy, were alike uncommon to me while in the jaws of slavery. The singing of a man cast

25   away upon a desolate island might be as appropriately considered as evidence of

26   contentment and happiness, as the singing of a slave; the songs of the one and of the other

27   are prompted by the same emotion.

24. The most common rhetorical device in this passage is:
     a. Analogy
     b. Parallelism
     c. Colloquialism
     d. Concrete Language
25. Which of the following is an example of personification:
     a. "Crying for joy"

b. "Jaws of slavery"

c. "Aching heart"

d. "Desolate island"

26. In line 7, "ineffable" most nearly means:
    a. Understandable
    b. Incomprehensible
    c. Horrible
    d. Mild

27. This passage is part of:
    a. An exposition
    b. An argument
    c. A narrative
    d. A description

28. The author's tone in this passage is:
    a. Educational
    b. Sad
    c. Angry
    d. Passionate

29. The purpose of this passage was to:
    a. Share a personal experience
    b. Convince the reader slavery was bad
    c. Convince the reader slavery was acceptable
    d. Entertain the reader

30. The following is an example of metaphor:
    a. "Impossible to conceive of a greater mistake"
    b. "Every tone was a testimony against slavery"
    c. "Those wild tones"
    d. "Prompted by the same emotion"

31. The singing of slaves is compared to:
    a. Singing with joy
    b. The singing of a man trapped on a desolate island
    c. Life on the plantation
    d. Allowance-day

32. The author uses figurative language to:
    a. Help the reader understand the plight of slaves
    b. Explain the composition of slave songs
    c. Make a political statement
    d. Share a religious viewpoint

33. The author credits the songs of slaves with:
    a. His own life as a slave
    b. His realization of the dehumanization of slavery
    c. His recognition of the lack of understanding in the north
    d. His emotional response

34. "They told a tale of woe which was then altogether beyond my feeble comprehension; they were tones loud, long, and deep; they breathed the prayer and complaint of souls boiling over with the bitterest anguish." This sentence illustrates:
    a. Anachronism
    b. Anathema
    c. Anaphora
    d. Parallelism

H.A. Guerber. Myths of the Norsemen.

1 The prime importance of the rude fragments of poetry preserved in early Icelandic
2 literature will now be disputed by none, but there has been until recent times an
3 extraordinary indifference to the wealth of religious tradition and mythical lore which they
4 contain.

5 The long neglect of these precious records of our heathen ancestors is not the fault of the
6 material in which all that survives of their religious beliefs is enshrined, for it may safely be
7 asserted that the Edda is as rich in the essentials of national romance and race-imagination,
8 rugged though it be, as the more graceful and idyllic mythology of the South. Neither is it
9 due to anything weak in the conception of the deities themselves, for although they may
10 not rise to great spiritual heights, foremost students of Icelandic literature agree that they
11 stand out rude and massive as the Scandinavian mountains. They exhibit "a spirit of victory,
12 superior to brute force, superior to mere matter, a spirit that fights and overcomes."1 "Even
13 were some part of the matter of their myths taken from others, yet the Norsemen have
14 given their gods a noble, upright, great spirit, and placed them upon a high level that is all
15 their own."2 "In fact these old Norse songs have a truth in them, an inward perennial truth
16 and greatness.It is a greatness not of mere body and gigantic bulk, but a rude greatness of
17 soul."3

18 The introduction of Christianity into the North brought with it the influence of the Classical
19 races, and this eventually supplanted the native genius, so that the alien mythology and
20 literature of Greece and Rome have formed an increasing part of the mental equipment of
21 the northern peoples in proportion as the native literature and tradition have been
22 neglected.

23 Undoubtedly Northern mythology has exercised a deep influence upon our customs, laws,
24 and language, and there has been, therefore, a great unconscious inspiration flowing from
25 these into English literature. The most distinctive traits of this mythology are a peculiar grim
26 humour, to be found in the religion of no other race, and a dark thread of tragedy which
27 runs throughout the whole woof, and these characteristics, touching both extremes, are
28 writ large over English literature.

29 But of conscious influence, compared with the rich draught of Hellenic inspiration, there is
30 little to be found, and if we turn to modern art the difference is even more apparent.

31 This indifference may be attributed to many causes, but it was due first to the fact that the
32 religious beliefs of our pagan ancestors were not held with any real tenacity. Hence the
33 success of the more or less considered policy of the early Christian missionaries to confuse
34 the heathen beliefs, and merge them in the new faith, an interesting example of which is to

35 be seen in the transference to the Christian festival of Easter of the attributes of the pagan
36 goddess Eástre, from whom it took even the name. Northern mythology was in this way
37 arrested ere it had attained its full development, and the progress of Christianity eventually
38 relegated it to the limbo of forgotten things. Its comprehensive and intelligent scheme,
39 however, in strong contrast with the disconnected mythology of Greece and Rome, formed
40 the basis of a more or less rational faith which prepared the Norseman to receive the
41 teaching of Christianity, and so helped to bring about its own undoing.

42 The religious beliefs of the North are not mirrored with any exactitude in the Elder Edda.
43 Indeed only a travesty of the faith of our ancestors has been preserved in Norse literature.
44 The early poet loved allegory, and his imagination rioted among the conceptions of his
45 fertile muse. "His eye was fixed on the mountains till the snowy peaks assumed human
46 features and the giant of the rock or the ice descended with heavy tread; or he would gaze
47 at the splendour of the spring, or of the summer fields, till Freya with the gleaming necklace
48 stepped forth, or Sif with the flowing locks of gold."4

49 We are told nothing as to sacrificial and religious rites, and all else is omitted which does
50 not provide material for artistic treatment. The so-called Northern Mythology, therefore,
51 may be regarded as a precious relic of the beginning of Northern poetry, rather than as a
52 representation of the religious beliefs of the Scandinavians, and these literary fragments
53 bear many signs of the transitional stage wherein the confusion of the old and new faiths is
54 easily apparent.

55 But notwithstanding the limitations imposed by long neglect it is possible to reconstruct in
56 part a plan of the ancient Norse beliefs, and the general reader will derive much profit from
57 Carlyle's illuminating study in "Heroes and Hero-worship." "A bewildering, inextricable
58 jungle of delusions, confusions, falsehoods and absurdities, covering the whole field of
59 Life!" he calls them, with all good reason. But he goes on to show, with equal truth,that at
60 the soul of this crude worship of distorted nature was a spiritual force seeking expression.
61 What we probe without reverence they viewed with awe, and not understanding it,
62 straightway deified it, as all children have been apt to do in all stages of the world's history.
63 Truly they were hero-worshippers after Carlyle's own heart, and scepticism had no place in
64 their simple philosophy.

65 It was the infancy of thought gazing upon a universe filled with divinity, and believing
66 heartily with all sincerity. A large-hearted people reaching out in the dark towards ideals
67 which were better than they knew. Ragnarok was to undo their gods because they had
68 stumbled from their higher standards.

69 We have to thank a curious phenomenon for the preservation of so much of the old lore as
70 we still possess. While foreign influences were corrupting the Norse language, it remained

practically unaltered in Iceland, which had been colonised from the mainland by the Norsemen who had fled thither to escape the oppression of Harold Fairhair after his crushing victory of Hafrsfirth. These people brought with them the poetic genius which had already manifested itself, and it took fresh root in that barren soil. Many of the old Norse poets were natives of Iceland, and in the early part of the Christian era, a supreme service was rendered to Norse literature by the Christian priest, Sæmund, who industriously brought together a large amount of pagan poetry in a collection known as the Elder Edda, which is the chief foundation of our present knowledge of the religion of our Norse ancestors. Icelandic literature remained a sealed book, however, until the end of the eighteenth century, and very slowly since that time it has been winning its way in the teeth of indifference, until there are now signs that it will eventually come into its own. "To know the old Faith," says Carlyle, "brings us into closer and clearer relation with the Past—with our own possessions in the Past. For the whole Past is the possession of the Present; the Past had always something true, and is a precious possession."

The weighty words of William Morris regarding the Volsunga Saga may also be fitly quoted as an introduction to the whole of this collection of "Myths of the Norsemen": "This is the great story of the North, which should be to all our race what the Tale of Troy was to the Greeks—to all our race first, and afterwards, when the change of the world has made our race nothing more than a name of what has been—a story too—then should it be to those that come after us no less than the Tale of Troy has been to us."

1 "Northern Mythology," Kauffmann.

2Halliday Sparling.

3Carlyle, "Heroes and Hero Worship."

4"Northern Mythology," Kauffmann.

35. Annotation is used to:
    a. Provide facts
    b. Make abstract thoughts concrete
    c. Provide references
    d. Share stories

36. In line 1, "rude" most closely means:
    a. Impolite
    b. Poorly written
    c. Incomplete
    d. Primitive

37. The "teeth of indifference" in lines 80-81 is an example of:
    a. Analogy
    b. Sarcasm
    c. Subjectivity
    d. Personification

38. Norse mythology is compared to:
    a. Icelandic mythology
    b. Greek mythology
    c. Christianity
    d. Danish mythology

39. Which of the following is an example of metaphor:
    a. "It took fresh root in that barren soil"
    b. "They had stumbled from their higher standards"
    c. "Spiritual force seeking expression"
    d. "Poetic genius"

40. The use of quotations is an example of:
    a. Ethos
    b. Pathos
    c. Logos
    d. Ad Hominem argument

41. What element is missing from the Elder Edda?
    a. Literary value
    b. Poetry
    c. Religious content
    d. Icelandic mythology

42. "His eye was fixed on the mountains till the snowy peaks assumed human features and the giant of the rock or the ice descended with heavy tread; or he would gaze at the splendour of the spring, or of the summer fields, till Freya with the gleaming necklace stepped forth, or Sif with the flowing locks of gold." is an example of:
    a. Alliteration
    b. Allegory
    c. Repetition
    d. Parody

43. In line 58, "jungle of delusions, confusions," is an example of:
    a. Euphony
    b. Cacophony
    c. Parallelism
    d. Anaphora

Sir Arthur Conan Doyle. The Lost World.

1   When we arrived at the hall we found a much greater concourse than I had expected. A line

2   of electric broughams discharged their little cargoes of white-bearded professors, while the

3   dark stream of humbler pedestrians, who crowded through the arched door-way, showed

4   that the audience would be popular as well as scientific. Indeed, it became evident to us as

5   soon as we had taken our seats that a youthful and even boyish spirit was abroad in the

6   gallery and the back portions of the hall. Looking behind me, I could see rows of faces of the

7   familiar medical student type. Apparently the great hospitals had each sent down their

8   contingent. The behavior of the audience at present was good-humored, but mischievous.

9   Scraps of popular songs were chorused with an enthusiasm which was a strange prelude to

10   a scientific lecture, and there was already a tendency to personal chaff which promised a

11   jovial evening to others, however embarrassing it might be to the recipients of these

12   dubious honors.

13   Thus, when old Doctor Meldrum, with his well-known curly-brimmed opera-hat, appeared

14   upon the platform, there was such a universal query of "Where DID you get that tile?" that

15   he hurriedly removed it, and concealed it furtively under his chair. When gouty Professor

16   Wadley limped down to his seat there were general affectionate inquiries from all parts of

17   the hall as to the exact state of his poor toe, which caused him obvious embarrassment. The

18   greatest demonstration of all, however, was at the entrance of my new acquaintance,

19   Professor Challenger, when he passed down to take his place at the extreme end of the

20   front row of the platform. Such a yell of welcome broke forth when his black beard first

21   protruded round the corner that I began to suspect Tarp Henry was right in his surmise, and

22   that this assemblage was there not merely for the sake of the lecture, but because it had

23   got rumored abroad that the famous Professor would take part in the proceedings.

24   There was some sympathetic laughter on his entrance among the front benches of well-

25   dressed spectators, as though the demonstration of the students in this instance was not

26   unwelcome to them. That greeting was, indeed, a frightful outburst of sound, the uproar of

27   the carnivora cage when the step of the bucket-bearing keeper is heard in the distance.

28   There was an offensive tone in it, perhaps, and yet in the main it struck me as mere riotous

29   outcry, the noisy reception of one who amused and interested them, rather than of one

30   they disliked or despised. Challenger smiled with weary and tolerant contempt, as a kindly

31   man would meet the yapping of a litter of puppies. He sat slowly down, blew out his chest,

32   passed his hand caressingly down his beard, and looked with drooping eyelids and

33   supercilious eyes at the crowded hall before him. The uproar of his advent had not yet died

34   away when Professor Ronald Murray, the chairman, and Mr. Waldron, the lecturer,

35   threaded their way to the front, and the proceedings began.

36 Professor Murray will, I am sure, excuse me if I say that he has the common fault of most
37 Englishmen of being inaudible. Why on earth people who have something to say which is
38 worth hearing should not take the slight trouble to learn how to make it heard is one of the
39 strange mysteries of modern life. Their methods are as reasonable as to try to pour some
40 precious stuff from the spring to the reservoir through a non-conducting pipe, which could
41 by the least effort be opened. Professor Murray made several profound remarks to his
42 white tie and to the water-carafe upon the table, with a humorous, twinkling aside to the
43 silver candlestick upon his right. Then he sat down, and Mr. Waldron, the famous popular
44 lecturer, rose amid a general murmur of applause. He was a stern, gaunt man, with a harsh
45 voice, and an aggressive manner, but he had the merit of knowing how to assimilate the
46 ideas of other men, and to pass them on in a way which was intelligible and even interesting
47 to the lay public, with a happy knack of being funny about the most unlikely objects, so that
48 the precession of the Equinox or the formation of a vertebrate became a highly humorous
49 process as treated by him.

50 It was a bird's-eye view of creation, as interpreted by science, which, in language always
51 clear and sometimes picturesque, he unfolded before us. He told us of the globe, a huge
52 mass of flaming gas, flaring through the heavens. Then he pictured the solidification, the
53 cooling, the wrinkling which formed the mountains, the steam which turned to water, the
54 slow preparation of the stage upon which was to be played the inexplicable drama of life.
55 On the origin of life itself he was discreetly vague. That the germs of it could hardly have
56 survived the original roasting was, he declared, fairly certain. Therefore it had come later.
57 Had it built itself out of the cooling, inorganic elements of the globe? Very likely. Had the
58 germs of it arrived from outside upon a meteor? It was hardly conceivable. On the whole,
59 the wisest man was the least dogmatic upon the point. We could not—or at least we had
60 not succeeded up to date in making organic life in our laboratories out of inorganic
61 materials. The gulf between the dead and the living was something which our chemistry
62 could not as yet bridge. But there was a higher and subtler chemistry of Nature, which,
63 working with great forces over long epochs, might well produce results which were
64 impossible for us. There the matter must be left.

44. "Then he pictured the solidification, the cooling, the wrinkling which formed the mountains, the steam which turned to water, the slow preparation of the stage upon which was to be played the inexplicable drama of life." This passage is an example of which rhetorical device?
    a. Parallelism
    b. Hyperbole
    c. Oxymoron
    d. Satire

45. Lines 36 to 41 illustrate the use of:
    a. Humor
    b. Irony
    c. Allegory
    d. Sarcasm

46. Which of the following is an example of figurative language?
    a. "formation of a vertebrate"
    b. "mysteries of modern life"
    c. "long epochs"
    d. "bird's-eye view of creation"

47. The author's intent is to:
    a. Educate
    b. Convince
    c. Entertain
    d. Oppose

48. The author's tone is:
    a. Playful
    b. Angry
    c. Serious
    d. Dramatic

49. "He was a stern, gaunt man, with a harsh voice, and an aggressive manner," is an example of the use of:
    a. Concrete language
    b. Abstract language
    c. Imagery
    d. Invective

50. What is the connotation of chaff?
    a. Insults
    b. Death
    c. Wheat
    d. Strength

51. "That greeting was, indeed, a frightful outburst of sound, the uproar of the carnivora cage when the step of the bucket-bearing keeper is heard in the distance." is an example of:
    a. Analogy
    b. Simile
    c. Description
    d. Exposition

52. The passage is a:
    a. Exposition
    b. Narrative
    c. Argument
    d. Anecdote

53. "Had it built itself out of the cooling, inorganic elements of the globe? Very likely. Had the germs of it arrived from outside upon a meteor? It was hardly conceivable." These are an example of what:
    a. Rhetorical questions
    b. Discussion questions
    c. Argumentative examples
    d. Comparisons

54. "As a kindly man would meet the yapping of a litter of puppies," is an example of:
    a. A simile
    b. A metaphor
    c. A rhetorical question
    d. An anecdote

55. This passage is most likely part of:
    a. A speech
    b. A novel
    c. An essay
    d. A debate

1

This passage is taken from John Burroughs' The Idyl of the Honey-bee. Read this passage and write an essay explaining how Burroughs' used language and rhetoric in his writing.

THERE is no creature with which man has surrounded himself that seems so much like a product of civilization, so much like the result of development on special lines and in special fields, as the honey-bee. Indeed, a colony of bees, with their neatness and love of order, their division of labor, their public-spiritedness, their thrift, their complex economies, and their inordinate love of gain, seems as far removed from a condition of rude nature as does a walled city or a cathedral town. Our native bee, on the other hand, the "burly, dozing humblebee," affects one more like the rude, untutored savage. He has learned nothing from experience. He lives from hand to mouth. He luxuriates in time of plenty, and he starves in times of scarcity. He lives in a rude nest, or in a hole in the ground, and in small communities; he builds a few deep cells or sacks in which he stores a little honey and bee-bread for his young, but as a worker in wax he is of the most primitive and awkward. The Indian regarded the honey-bee as an ill-omen. She was the white man's fly. In fact she was the epitome of the white man himself. She has the white man's craftiness, his industry, his architectural skill, his neatness and love of system, his foresight; and, above all, his eager, miserly habits. The honey-bee's great ambition is to be rich, to lay up great stores, to possess the sweet of every flower that blooms. She is more than provident. Enough will not satisfy her; she must have all she can get by hook or by crook. She comes from the oldest country, Asia, and thrives best in the most fertile and long-settled lands.

Yet the fact remains that the honey-bee is essentially a wild creature, and never has been and cannot be thoroughly domesticated. Its proper home is the woods, and thither every new swarm counts on going; and thither many do go in spite of the care and watchfulness of the bee-keeper. If the woods in any given locality are deficient in trees with suitable cavities, the bees resort to all sorts of makeshifts; they go into chimneys, into barns and out-houses, under stones, into rocks, and so forth. Several chimneys in my locality with disused flues are taken possession of by colonies of bees nearly every season. One day, while bee-hunting, I developed a line that went toward a farmhouse where I had reason to believe no bees were kept. I followed it up and questioned the farmer about his bees. He said he kept no bees, but that a swarm had taken possession of his chimney, and another had gone under the clapboards in the gable end of his house. He had taken a large lot of honey out of both places the year before. Another farmer told me that one day his family had seen a number of bees examining a knothole in the side of his house; the next day, as they were sitting down to dinner, their attention was attracted by a loud humming noise, when they discovered a swarm of bees settling upon the side of the house and pouring into the knothole. In subsequent years other swarms came to the same place.

Apparently every swarm of bees, before it leaves the parent hive, sends out exploring parties to look up the future home. The woods and groves are searched through and through, and no doubt the privacy of many a squirrel and many a wood-mouse is intruded upon. What cozy nooks and retreats they do spy out, so much more attractive than the painted hive in the garden, so much cooler in summer and so much warmer in winter!

This short excerpt, taken from Walt Whitman's Preface to Leaves of Grass, discusses the writer's perception of America and the American people. Your argumentative essay should refute, support or qualify this text and his interpretation of America.

AMERICA does not repel the past, or what the past has produced under its forms, or amid other politics, or the idea of castes, or the old religions—accepts the lesson with calmness—is not impatient because the slough still sticks to opinions and manners in literature, while the life which served its requirements has passed into the new life of the new forms—perceives that the corpse is slowly borne from the eating and sleeping rooms of the house—perceives that it waits a little while in the door—that it was fittest for its days—that its action has descended to the stalwart and well-shaped heir who approaches—and that he shall be fittest for his days.

The Americans of all nations at any time upon the earth, have probably the fullest poetical nature. The United States themselves are essentially the greatest poem. In the history of the earth hitherto, the largest and most stirring appear tame and orderly to their ampler largeness and stir. Here at last is something in the doings of man that corresponds with the broadcast doings of the day and night. Here is action untied from strings, necessarily blind to particulars and details, magnificently moving in masses. Here is the hospitality which for ever indicates heroes. Here the performance, disdaining the trivial, unapproach'd in the tremendous audacity of its crowds and groupings, and the push of its perspective, spreads with crampless and flowing breadth, and showers its prolific and splendid extravagance. One sees it must indeed own the riches of the summer and winter, and need never be bankrupt while corn grows from the ground, or the orchards drop apples, or the bays contain fish, or men beget children upon women.

Other states indicate themselves in their deputies—but the genius of the United States is not best or most in its executives or legislatures, nor in its ambassadors or authors, or colleges or churches or parlors, nor even in its newspapers or inventors—but always most in the common people, south, north, west, east, in all its States, through all its mighty amplitude. The largeness of the nation, however, were monstrous without a corresponding largeness and generosity of the spirit of the citizen. Not swarming states, nor streets and steamships, nor prosperous business, nor farms, nor capital, nor learning, may suffice for the ideal of man—nor suffice the poet. No reminiscences may suffice either. A live nation can always cut a deep mark, and can have the best authority the cheapest—namely, from its own soul. This is the sum of the profitable uses of individuals or states, and of present action and grandeur, and of the subjects of poets. (As if it were necessary to trot back generation after generation to the eastern records! As if the beauty and sacredness of the demonstrable must fall behind that of the mythical! As if men do not make their mark out of any times! As if the opening of the western continent by discovery, and what has transpired in North and South America, were less than the small theater of the antique, or the aimless sleep-walking of the middle ages!) The pride of the United States leaves the wealth and finesse of the cities, and all returns of commerce and agriculture, and all the magnitude of geography or shows of exterior victory, to enjoy the sight and realization of full-sized men, or one full-sized man unconquerable and simple.

These three pieces speak to McCarthyism and Cold War fears in the 1950s. Synthesize all three of these writings to analyze the impact of McCarthyism, both then and now.

Joseph McCarthy, Wheeling, Virginia, 1950

Five years after a world war has been won, men's hearts should anticipate a long peace—and men's minds should be free from the heavy weight that comes with war. But this is not such a period—for this is not a period of peace. This is a time of "the cold war." This is a time when all the world is split into two vast, increasingly hostile armed camps—a time of a great armament race.

Today we can almost physically hear the mutterings and rumblings of an invigorated god of war. You can see it, feel it, and hear it all the way from the Indochina hills, from the shores of Formosa, right over into the very heart of Europe itself.

The one encouraging thing is that the "mad moment" has not yet arrived for the firing of the gun or the exploding of the bomb which will set civilization about the final task of destroying itself. There is still a hope for peace if we finally decide that no longer can we safely blind our eyes and close our ears to those facts which are shaping up more and more clearly . . . and that is that we are now engaged in a show-down fight . . . not the usual war between nations for land areas or other material gains, but a war between two diametrically opposed ideologies.

The great difference between our western Christian world and the atheistic Communist world is not political, gentlemen, it is moral. For instance, the Marxian idea of confiscating the land and factories and running the entire economy as a single enterprise is momentous. Likewise, Lenin's invention of the one-party police state as a way to make Marx's idea work is hardly less momentous.

Stalin's resolute putting across of these two ideas, of course, did much to divide the world. With only these differences, however, the east and the west could most certainly still live in peace.

The real, basic difference, however, lies in the religion of immoralism . . . invented by Marx, preached feverishly by Lenin, and carried to unimaginable extremes by Stalin. This religion of immoralism, if the Red half of the world triumphs—and well it may, gentlemen—this religion of immoralism will more deeply wound and damage mankind than any conceivable economic or political system.

Karl Marx dismissed God as a hoax, and Lenin and Stalin have added in clear-cut, unmistakable language their resolve that no nation, no people who believe in a god, can exist side by side with their communistic state.

Karl Marx, for example, expelled people from his Communist Party for mentioning such things as love, justice, humanity or morality. He called this "soulful ravings" and "sloppy sentimentality." . . .

Today we are engaged in a final, all-out battle between communistic atheism and Christianity. The modern champions of communism have selected this as the time, and ladies and gentlemen, the chips are down—they are truly down.

Edward R. Murrow. Response to Joseph McCarthy.

I have worked for CBS for more than 19 years. The company has subscribed fully to my integrity and responsibility as a broadcaster and as a loyal American. I require no lectures from the junior Senator from Wisconsin as to the dangers or terrors of Communism. Having watched the aggressive forces at work in Western Europe, having had friends in Eastern Europe butchered and driven into exile, having broadcast from London in 1943 that the Russians were responsible for the Katyn massacre, having told the story of the Russian refusal to let Allied aircraft to land on Russian fields after dropping supplies to those who rose in Warsaw and then were betrayed by the Russians, and having been denounced by the Russian radio for these reports, I cannot feel that I require instruction from the Senator on the evils of Communism.

Having searched my conscience and my files, I cannot contend that I have always been right or wise. But I have attempted to pursue the truth with some diligence and to report it, even though, as in this case, I had been warned in advance that I would be subjected to the attentions of Senator McCarthy.

We shall hope to deal with matters of more -- more vital interest for the country next week.

Senator Margaret Chase Smith. National Suicide. 1950

Mr. President, I would like to speak briefly and simply about a serious national condition. It is a national feeling of fear and frustration that could result in national suicide and the end of everything that we Americans hold dear. It is a condition that comes from the lack of effective leadership in either the legislative branch or the executive branch of our Government.

That leadership is so lacking that serious and responsible proposals are being made that national advisory commissions be appointed to provide such critically needed leadership.

I speak as briefly as possible because too much harm has already been done with irresponsible words of bitterness and selfish political opportunism. I speak as simply as possible because the issue is too great to be obscured by eloquence. I speak simply and briefly in the hope that my words will be taken to heart.

I speak as a Republican. I speak as a woman. I speak as a United States Senator. I speak as an American.

The United States Senate has long enjoyed worldwide respect as the greatest deliberative body in the world. But recently that deliberative character has too often been debased to the level of a forum of hate and character assassination sheltered by the shield of congressional immunity.

It is ironical that we Senators can debate in the Senate directly or indirectly, by any form of words impute to any American, who is not a Senator, any conduct or motive unworthy or unbecoming an American—and without that non-Senator American having any legal redress against it—yet if we say the same thing in the Senate about our colleagues we can be stopped on the grounds of being out of order.

It is strange that we can verbally attack anyone else without restraint and with full protection and yet we hold ourselves above the same type of criticism here on the Senate floor. Surely the United States Senate is big enough to take self-criticism and self-appraisal. Surely we should be able to take the same kind of character attacks that we "dish out" to outsiders.

I think that it is high time for the United States Senate and its Members to do some soul searching—for us to weigh our consciences—on the manner in which we are performing our duty to the people of America; on the manner in which we are using or abusing our individual powers and privileges.

I think that it is high time that we remembered that we have sworn to uphold and defend the Constitution. I think that it is high time that we remembered that the Constitution, as amended, speaks not only of the freedom of speech, but also of trial by jury instead of trial by accusation.

Whether it be a criminal prosecution in court or a character prosecution in the Senate, there is little practical distinction when the life of a person has been ruined.

Those of us who shout the loudest about Americanism in making character assassinations are all too frequently those who, by our own words and acts, ignore some of the basic principles of Americanism—

The right to criticize;

The right to hold unpopular beliefs;

The right to protest;

The right of independent thought.

The exercise of these rights should not cost one single American citizen his reputation or his right to a livelihood nor should he be in danger of losing his reputation or livelihood merely because he happens to know someone who holds unpopular beliefs. Who of us doesn't? Otherwise none of us could call our souls our own. Otherwise thought control would have set in.

Practice Test 2 Answer Key

1. a	2. a	3. a	4. b	5. b	6. a
7. c	8. d	9. c	10. a	11. b	12. a
13. b	14. d	15. d	16. a	17. a	18. b
19. b	20. b	21. c	22. d	23. a	24. b
25. b	26. b	27. c	28. b	29. a	30. b
31. b	32. a	33. b	34. d	35. c	36. d
37. d	38. b	39. a	40. a	41. c	42. b
43. d	44. b	45. a	46. d	47. c	48. a
49. c	50. a	51. a	52. b	53. a	54. a
55. b					

Expository Essay 2

John Burroughs' "An Idle of the Honey-Bee" creates a comprehensive analogy, comparing the honeybee to human civilization. While the essay may be thematically focused on honeybees, the author intends to make statements about both bees and people, creating a broader look at society. In this piece, Burroughs relies upon a variety of figurative examples to create a single metaphor.

The honeybee is, according to Burroughs, very much like the ideal urban householder. It builds homes, maintains social organization and order, and works together productively. The bees are efficient and practical, presenting an idealized look at human society. The honeybees, working together in their hives, are like a community in a walled town, working toward shared goals and aspirations. Burroughs' town, his notions of civilization, it must be noted, are entirely western. His analogy works only because it is specific to his opinion and perspective.

The industry and practicality of the honeybee is contrasted with the lowly "humblebee". This bee does not work hard, live neatly or strive to create a reserve of honey. The everyday bee simply does the minimum required to survive and reproduce, nothing more. In this, the "humblebee," today's bumblebee, is compared to the uneducated, living hand to mouth with no hopes of anything more. Given Burroughs' later discussion of the responses of native peoples to the honeybee, it seems that he likely intended his analogy to link the humblebee to native peoples, not yet civilized by Europeans.

The productivity and care of the honeybee extends beyond the walls of its own hive. The honeybee seeks out the best homes and sends scouts in search of new ones. In this, we can model ourselves after the honeybee. While this analogy may have been, in Burroughs' mind, a positive one, today it seems much less so. He refers to the impressions of native peoples, colonized by honeybee-bearing Europeans. They found the bees to be pests, an ill-omen. The order, the providence, even the thrift of the bees reflected that of the settlers in their lands. Just as the bees are not content with the nectar of a single flower, so too the new colonists were not content with just a portion of what they came across. Instead, the civilization of the bees, over time, took over that of the natives, whether they be people or bumblebees.

The bee may be domestic, but it has not been domesticated. It retains the ability to make different choices , just as we do. For the bee, these choices are adaptive. When nowhere suitable is easily available, the bees will make do with different options, like a chimney. This too, reflects the human possibility for innovation, as part of Burroughs' metaphor.

The use of rhetorical devices, particularly analogy and metaphor, in this text suggest the ability of a skilled author to create broad comparisons, but they also illustrate the flaw in those comparisons. To the modern reader, while you might see a comparison between the walled town and the honeybee hive, the texts implied value judgments reveal it as a product of its time and place.

Argumentative Essay 2

Whitman's argument in this text is rather simple; the people make up the essence of America. His language is poetic and figurative, but his point is accessible. This simple notion holds as true today as it did in the 19th century. While lives have changed dramatically during the intervening 150 years, the fundamental nature of America is still driven by its citizens, not its cities or politics.

In order to define America, Whitman first defines what it is not defined by, including old religion, castes and history. These concepts are even compared to a rotting corpse, something repugnant and to be avoided, buried deeply beneath the soil. America emerges from this old history. Today's America is quite far removed from its colonial origins as a young nation, but it was not for Whitman. We can, in a sense, recognize the analogy comparing the old to the dead and contrasting it with the strong and the new. The America of today, is perhaps, less new than it once was. Today, we can look toward other young nations, new democracies, casting off their own corpses in favor of a new beginning driven by the people.

America's wealth and bounty are, for Whitman, its people. They are warm and hospitable, driven by goodness, for Whitman, rather than rules. Whitman's vision of America remains, in some ways, true even today. Our news is filled with stories of assistance offered and accepted, groups joining together to help those in need, and the value of community. Community is, of course, made up of these same, common Americans.

Whitman specifies that it is not the powerful who drive the nation to greatness. It is not the government, the educators or the inventors. It is the common people, the working people. Later in the 19th century, the common people fought for women's suffrage and worker's rights. Long after Whitman's time, it was the common people that drove essential social movements, like the civil rights movement. Even today, the common people, the everyday people, continue to push for social change. While social change may seem modern, we cannot forget that the very foundations of America rested on this same social change, driven by the common person.

Walt Whitman's notion is a romantic and poetic one, but not one entirely distant from today's reality. While our world may largely be ruled by the few, the daily interactions with the many remain a defining force across America. Again and again, across the world, the actions of the common people, of the many rather than the few, can bring about great change within communities.

Synthesis Essay 2

U.S. Senator Joe McCarthy is one of the most remembered figures of the Cold War. During the post-World War II years, the country feared the growth of communism throughout the Soviet Union and Eastern Europe. While the most significant communist presence was far away from U.S. shores, some, including McCarthy, feared that communism was much closer. McCarthy saw communism in the intellectuals, the artists, the filmmakers and movie stars of America. Creating his own witch hunt, McCarthy interrogated, tried and convicted individuals of nothing more than the freedom of speech. These three passages mark the beginning of McCarthyism, a press response, and a political response.

McCarthy's argument in Wheeling, Virginia was an emotional one. He wanted to rouse the listener to fear. They were to fear not only the communists far away who wanted to take their property and their freedom, but also communists closer to home. He relies on pathos for his argument. There is no other alternative, as there is neither a logical nor authoritative basis for McCarthy's actions.

Well-known journalist Edward R. Murrow responded to McCarthy's accusations in a personal way. He was angry, frustrated, but still clearly spoken. His response specifically addressed McCarthy, but also identified his response as a waste of time, telling his listeners that he hoped to have news to report the following week. He offers his own exposition on communism, talking about his reporting and concrete, personal experiences with communism, rather than some distant and fear-invoking idea. If McCarthy's argument relied on pathos, Murrow's relies on logos. Senator Chase spoke specifically about personal freedoms, and the denial of freedoms that had occurred under McCarthy. Chase does not speak of her own experiences, but from the authority of the U.S. Constitution.

McCarthy's is a straw man argument. He does not rely upon facts, but fear. He uses figurative language to invoke fear in his reader. Here, figurative language takes the place of facts, obscuring the very lack of those facts. Certainly, the U.S. was at risk from the Soviet Union during the Cold War, but he does not deal in the realities. He wants the support of his listeners and so he taps into their emotions, not their sense of reason. While McCarthy's argument was fundamentally flawed, it was also successful. McCarthyism destroyed the careers of many, as those in a wide variety of fields were deemed communists, because they had once been known to associate with someone who was or wasn't, as the case might be.

These arguments remain current and relevant today. Senator Chase's reminders of personal freedom speak to the modern reader, but the fear-mongering found in McCarthy's words may also be familiar. The political climate today seems surprisingly unchanged as the same rhetorical tools remain in play. While some are willing to deal in facts and authority, others continue to tap into emotions to avoid essential issues or to gain support where it has not been earned.

Practice Test 3

A.H. Lane Fox. Primitive Warfare.

1 `Is not the world at the present time, and has it not always been, the scene of a continuous
2 progress? Have not the arts grown up from an obscure origin, and is not this growth
3 continuing to the present day?

4 This is the question which lies at the very threshold of our subject, and we must endeavour
5 to treat it by the light of evidence alone, apart from all considerations of a traditional or
6 poetic character.

7 I do not propose here to enter into a disquisition upon the functions of the human mind.
8 But it must I think be admitted, that if man possessed from the first the same nature that
9 belongs to him at the present time, he must at the commencement of his career in this
10 world have been destitute of all creative power. The mind has never been endowed with
11 any creative faculty. The only powers we possess are those of digesting, adapting, and
12 applying, by the intellectual faculties, the experience acquired through the medium of the
13 senses. We come into the world helpless and speechless, possessing only in common with
14 the brutes such instincts as are necessary for the bare sustenance of life under the most
15 facile conditions; all that follows afterwards is dependent purely on experience.

16 Whether we afterwards become barbarous or civilized, whether we follow a hunting,
17 nomadic, or agricultural life, whether we embrace this religion or that, or attain proficiency
18 in any of the arts, all this is dependent purely on the accident of our birth, which places us
19 in a position to build upon the experience of our ancestors, adding to it the experience
20 acquired by ourselves. For although it is doubtless true that the breeds of mankind, like the
21 breeds of our domestic animals, by continual cultivation during many generations, have
22 improved, and that by this means races have been produced capable of being educated to a
23 higher degree than those which have remained uncivilized, this does not alter the fact that
24 it is by experience alone, conscious or unconscious, self-imposed or compulsory, and by a
25 process of slow and laborious induction, that we arrive at the degree of perfection to which,
26 according to our opportunities and our relative endowments, we ultimately attain.

27 The amount, therefore, which any one individual or any one generation is capable of adding
28 to the civilization of their age must be immeasurably small, in comparison with what they
29 derive from it.

30 I could not perhaps appeal to an audience more capable of appreciating the truth of these
31 remarks than to the members of an Institution, the object of which is to examine into the

32 improvements and so-called inventions which are from time to time effected in the
33 machinery and implements of war.

34 How often does any proposal or improvement come before this Institution which after
35 investigating its antecedents is found to possess originality of design? Is it not a fact that
36 even the most ingenious and successful inventions turn out on inquiry to be mere
37 adaptations of contrivances already existing, or that they are produced by applying to one
38 branch of industry the principles or the contrivances which have been evolved in another. I
39 think that no one can have constantly attended the lectures of this or any similar Institution,
40 without becoming impressed, above all things, with the want of originality observable
41 amongst men, and with the great calls which, even in this age of cultivated intellects and
42 abundant materials to work upon, all inventors are obliged to make upon those who have
43 preceded them.

44 Since, then, we ourselves are so entirely creatures of education, and derive so little from
45 our own unaided resources, it follows that the first created man, if similarly constituted,
46 having no antecedents from which to derive instruction, could not, without external aid,
47 have made any material or rapid advance towards the initiation of the arts.

48 So fully has the truth of this been recognized by those who are not themselves advocates
49 for the theory of development, that in order to account for the very first stages of human
50 progress they have found it necessary to assume the hypothesis of supernatural agency:
51 such we know was the belief of the classical pagan nations, who attributed the origin of
52 many of the arts to their gods; such we know to be the tradition of many savage and semi-
53 civilized nations of modern times that have attained to the first stages of culture. But we
54 have already disposed of this hypothesis at the commencement of these remarks, by
55 deciding that our arguments should be based solely upon evidence. We are, therefore,
56 under the necessity of assuming, in the absence of any evidence to the contrary, that none
57 but the agencies which help us now were at the disposal of our first ancestors, and the
58 alternative to which we must have recourse is that of supposing that the progress of those
59 days was immeasurably slower than it is at present, and that vast ages must have elapsed
60 after the first appearance of man before he began to show even the first indications of a
61 settled advance.

62 Yet the complex civilization of our own time has been built on the foundations that were
63 laid by these aborigines of our species, while the brute creation may be said to have
64 produced little more than was necessary to their own wants or those of their immediate
65 offspring. Man has been the agent employed in a work of continuous progression.
66 Generation has succeeded generation, and race has succeeded race, each contributing its
67 quota to the fabrication of the edifice, and then giving place to other workmen. But the

68 progress of the edifice itself has never ceased; it has gone on, I maintain (contrary to the
69 opinion of some writers of our day), always in fulfilment of one vast design. It is a work of all
70 time.

1. The first paragraph illustrates the use of:
   a. Parallelism
   b. Pathos
   c. Logos
   d. Rhetorical questions

2. Which of the following is an example of figurative language?
   a. Threshold of our subject
   b. Functions of the human mind
   c. Complex civilization
   d. Fulfilment of one vast design

3. In line 15, "facile" most likely means:
   a. Easy
   b. Difficult
   c. Favorable
   d. Friendly

4. What is the most correct statement regarding the author's perspective or point of view on race?
   a. He believes that all races are equal.
   b. He believes in the superiority of one race over another.
   c. He makes no statements about race.
   d. He believes all people have equal potential.

5. This piece was originally written for an audience of:
   a. Scholars
   b. Students
   c. Children
   d. The general public

6. This author's primary rhetorical device or fallacy is:
   a. Argument from ignorance
   b. Logos
   c. Begging the question
   d. Pathos

7. In lines 16 and 17, "hunting, nomadic, or agricultural life" is an example of:
   a. Parallelism
   b. Anachronism
   c. Chronological order
   d. Connotation

8. The author attempts to refute what argument:
   a. We are born with knowledge.
   b. We are born without knowledge.
   c. Humans were created by a supernatural being.
   d. Humans were not created by a supernatural being.

9. "We are, therefore, under the necessity of assuming, in the absence of any evidence to the contrary, that none but the agencies which help us now were at the disposal of our first ancestors" is an example of:
   a. An ad hominem argument
   b. An argument from ignorance
   c. False dichotomy
   d. Red herring

1   The drug therapy of the magicians actually utilized everything under the sun as a remedy.
2   The more out of the way and the less suitable for a remedy a substance seemed to be, the
3   more likely it was to be chosen by the magician intent upon healing. For it was always the
4   main object of these practising quacks to make their treatment as sensational as possible. In
5   this they succeeded best by employing the most extraordinary substances as remedies.
6   Thus they made use of gold, silver, precious stones and pearls, just because these, owing to
7   their value, were held in great esteem, and their medical application, therefore, was bound
8   to create a sensation. But the most loathsome substances were quite as readily employed,
9   for here, too, the most general attention was bound to be attracted by their application.
10   Human feces, urine, and menstrual blood were introduced into the materia medica in such
11   a manner. The awe with which parts of corpses usually inspired the non-medical part of the
12   public was relied upon by the magicians to advertise their cures. Thus these quacks
13   administered powders of human bones to the ailing.

14   But inasmuch as what is conspicuous and unusual has always enjoyed an especial esteem
15   with humanity, the incredible remedies of the magicians naturally found everywhere an
16   abundance of believers; and as particularly the most nonsensical theory is most tenacious of
17   life, provided it has been presented in apparent combination with the miraculous, the
18   medical armamentarium rapidly took on a very peculiar aspect. Until the present more
19   modern times medicine was condemned to the encumbrance of this rubbish, this list of odd
20   and loathsome remedies, whose admission to the pharmacopœia was only due to the whim
21   of a human mind that constantly hankers after the extraordinary and the miraculous.

22   Finally the magic observances to which the magicians resorted in the treatment of the sick,
23   have shown a remarkable vitality, for they are in vogue even in modern times, and many
24   sections of our people even to-day swear unconditionally by the curative efficacy of various
25   agencies which demonstratively have been derived from the medicine of the magicians. But
26   now such agencies are no longer ascribed to magic or sorcery, but they are called "cures by
27   means of sympathy." And as many modern people believe that various incomprehensible
28   mystic performances cause certain mysterious powers, otherwise absolutely unknown, to
29   exert a curative influence upon certain diseases, so did the ancients believe exactly the
30   same. This was the origin of exorcism as a remedy for disease. Exorcism played a
31   conspicuous part in the middle ages as a means of stopping hemorrhages, and even in these
32   modern times, as is well-known, this method of cure finds many adherents.

33   This magic treatment was believed to be especially efficacious if the exorcisms had been
34   written or engraved upon paper, gold, precious stones, etc., in which case they were

35 suspended around the neck of the patient. Countless talismans (from the Arabic *tilsam*,
36 magic image) and amulets (from the Arabic *hamalet*, trinket) were thus manufactured, and
37 even to our own time there are survivals of this medical superstition. Altho these mystic
38 observances are performed in various ways, and their modifications are practically
39 innumerable, yet certain radical resemblances are continually appearing among the magic
40 rites of the most diverse races, and some of these practises have even persisted up to the
41 present time. Thus the rope of the hung criminal plays a conspicuous part in antique magic
42 as well as in modern sympathy treatment; the same importance is attributed to shooting-
43 stars, to the moon, to crossroads, to certain numerals, such as 3, 7, 9, etc. It is a highly
44 interesting fact that such conceptions, as remarkable for their therapeutical associations as
45 for their crass superstition, are possessed of a vitality which persists for centuries. Peoples,
46 religions, philosophical systems, political revolutions have risen and vanished, but the belief
47 in the curative action of the rope of a hung criminal or the therapeutic significance of the
48 crossroad has survived. The mystic influence which is exerted by the numerals 3, 7, 9, and
49 still more so by the dreadful 13, upon the life and health of man, haunts the minds of the
50 multitude in this century of physical enlightenment exactly as it did in remote antiquity. But
51 we can not here enter into the reason for these interesting facts, and we must refer those
52 who desire more detailed information on this subject to the voluminous literature of
53 superstition.

54 Furthermore, the belief in magic cures was not more prevalent among the ancient
55 professors of medicine than among the laity, and even the most prominent practitioners
56 were not able to emancipate themselves from this belief. Galen, for instance, who, as is
57 well-known, mastered the entire literature of antique medicine as none before or after him
58 has ever done, openly avows his belief in the efficacy of magic cures, and, what is more
59 remarkable, Galen in this respect has changed from a Saul to a Paul. He ruefully recalled,
60 later, the condemnatory decree which he had originally promulgated regarding the magic
61 treatment of the sick. Let us call to mind how he expresses himself in his essay on medical
62 treatment in Homer: "Many, as I have done for a long time, believe that conjurations
63 resemble the fairy tales of old women. But gradually, and from the observation of obvious
64 facts, I have come to the conclusion that power is exercised by them; for I have learned to
65 know their advantages in stings of scorpions, and also in bones which became lodged in the
66 throat, and which were at once coughed up as a result of conjuration. Many remedies are
67 excellent in every respect, and magic formulæ answer their purpose" ("Alexander of
68 Tralles," Book 11, Chapter I., Vol. II., page 477). One of the most prominent post-Galenian
69 physicians also, Alexander of Tralles, openly avows, with reference to this utterance of
70 Galen, that he himself is a believer in magic cures, and he says: "If the great Galen, as well
71 as many other physicians of ancient times, bear witness to this fact (the efficacy of magic

72 treatment of the sick), why shall we not impart to you what we have learned from our own
73 experience and what we have heard from trustworthy friends?" ("Alexander of
74 Tralles,"*ibid.*). Accordingly, his Βιβλία Ἰατρικά was filled with enumerations of the most
75 various magical cures. But, now, if the classics of antique medicine have proven themselves
76 to be so friendly to the medical science of magicians, what was the condition of the mind,
77 then, of the average physician of ancient times? Is it astonishing if young and old, high and
78 low, without distinction, were blind adherents of magical medicine? Thus medical literature
79 of the last century, B.C., and especially that of the centuries from the Christian era until late
80 in the middle ages, was an actual treasury of conjuration and other mummeries. This
81 description applies specifically to the "Materia Medica" of Quintus Serenus Samonicus,
82 written in hexameters. It is true, the magical sequel to this book entailed painful
83 consequences on the writer, for the emperor Caracalla had the poor author executed (Ael.
84 Spartian., "Caracalla," Chapter IV., § 4) merely, as it is reported, because he dared to advise
85 in his works as a remedy against intermittent fever the wearing of amulets, a medical
86 expedient which had been prohibited by the emperor himself.

10. Parenthetical notes throughout this passage are an example of:
    a. Annotation
    b. Connotation
    c. Cacophony
    d. Aphorism

11. In line 1, "everything under the sun" is an example of:
    a. A metaphor
    b. A cliche
    c. A simile
    d. An analogy

12. "Galen in this respect has changed from a Saul to a Paul." is an example of:
    a. Personification
    b. Allegory
    c. Allusion
    d. Anachronism

13. This work is primarily:
    a. Argumentative
    b. Persuasive
    c. Narrative
    d. Expository

14. The author occasionally uses which of these rhetorical tools?
    a. Rhetorical questions
    b. Personification
    c. Euphony
    d. Irony

15. "Mummeries" most nearly means:
    e. Magic tricks
    f. Illusions
    g. Performances
    h. Miracles

16. "Emancipate" most closely means:
    a. Free
    b. Bind
    c. Engage
    d. Loosen

17. What is the connotation of "blind adherents"?
    a. Supporter
    b. Unthinking supporters
    c. Thoughtful supporters
    d. Supporters who could not see

18. The following, "conjurations resemble the fairy tales of old women," is an example of:
    a. An anachronism
    b. An analogy
    c. An allegory
    d. A simile

Washington Irving. John Bull.

1　THERE is no species of humor in which the English more excel, than that which consists in
2　caricaturing and giving ludicrous appellations, or nicknames. In this way they have
3　whimsically designated, not merely individuals, but nations; and, in their fondness for
4　pushing a joke, they have not spared even themselves. One would think that, in
5　personifying itself, a nation would be apt to picture something grand, heroic and imposing,
6　but it is characteristic of the peculiar humor of the English, and of their love for what is
7　blunt, comic, and familiar, that they have embodied their national oddities in the figure of a
8　sturdy, corpulent old fellow, with a three-cornered hat, red waistcoat, leather breeches,
9　and stout oaken cudgel. Thus they have taken a singular delight in exhibiting their most
10　private foibles in a laughable point of view; and have been so successful in their
11　delineations, that there is scarcely a being in actual existence more absolutely present to
12　the public mind than that eccentric personage, John Bull.

13　Perhaps the continual contemplation of the character thus drawn of them has contributed
14　to fix it upon the nation; and thus to give reality to what at first may have been painted in a
15　great measure from the imagination. Men are apt to acquire peculiarities that are
16　continually ascribed to them. The common orders of English seem wonderfully captivated
17　with the *beau ideal* which they have formed of John Bull, and endeavor to act up to the
18　broad caricature that is perpetually before their eyes. Unluckily, they sometimes make their
19　boasted Bull-ism an apology for their prejudice or grossness; and this I have especially
20　noticed among those truly homebred and genuine sons of the soil who have never migrated
21　beyond the sound of Bow-bells. If one of these should be a little uncouth in speech, and apt
22　to utter impertinent truths, he confesses that he is a real John Bull, and always speaks his
23　mind. If he now and then flies into an unreasonable burst of passion about trifles, he
24　observes, that John Bull is a choleric old blade, but then his passion is over in a moment,
25　and he bears no malice. If he betrays a coarseness of taste, and an insensibility to foreign
26　refinements, he thanks heaven for his ignorance—he is a plain John Bull, and has no relish
27　for frippery and nicknacks. His very proneness to be gulled by strangers, and to pay
28　extravagantly for absurdities, is excused under the plea of munificence—for John is always
29　more generous than wise.

30　Thus, under the name of John Bull, he will contrive to argue every fault into a merit, and will
31　frankly convict himself of being the honestest fellow in existence.

32　However little, therefore, the character may have suited in the first instance, it has
33　gradually adapted itself to the nation, or rather they have adapted themselves to each
34　other; and a stranger who wishes to study English peculiarities, may gather much valuable
35　information from the innumerable portraits of John Bull, as exhibited in the windows of the

36 caricature-shops. Still, however, he is one of those fertile humorists, that are continually
37 throwing out new portraits, and presenting different aspects from different points of view;
38 and, often as he has been described, I cannot resist the temptation to give a slight sketch of
39 him, such as he has met my eye.

40 John Bull, to all appearance, is a plain downright matter-of-fact fellow, with much less of
41 poetry about him than rich prose. There is little of romance in his nature, but a vast deal of
42 strong natural feeling. He excels in humor more than in wit; is jolly rather than gay;
43 melancholy rather than morose; can easily be moved to a sudden tear, or surprised into a
44 broad laugh; but he loathes sentiment, and has no turn for light pleasantry. He is a boon
45 companion, if you allow him to have his humor, and to talk about himself; and he will stand
46 by a friend in a quarrel, with life and purse, however soundly he may be cudgeled.

47 In this last respect, to tell the truth, he has a propensity to be somewhat too ready. He is a
48 busy-minded personage, who thinks not merely for himself and family, but for all the
49 country round, and is most generously disposed to be everybody's champion. He is
50 continually volunteering his services to settle his neighbors' affairs, and takes it in great
51 dudgeon if they engage in any matter of consequence without asking his advice; though he
52 seldom engages in any friendly office of the kind without finishing by getting into a squabble
53 with all parties, and then railing bitterly at their ingratitude. He unluckily took lessons in his
54 youth in the noble science of defense, and having accomplished himself in the use of his
55 limbs and his weapons, and become a perfect master at boxing and cudgel-play, he has had
56 a troublesome life of it ever since. He cannot hear of a quarrel between the most distant of
57 his neighbors, but he begins incontinently to fumble with the head of his cudgel, and
58 consider whether his interest or honor does not require that he should meddle in the broil.
59 Indeed he has extended his relations of pride and policy so completely over the whole
60 country, that no event can take place, without infringing some of his finely-spun rights and
61 dignities. Couched in his little domain, with these filaments stretching forth in every
62 direction, he is like some choleric, bottle-bellied old spider, who has woven his web over a
63 whole chamber, so that a fly cannot buzz, nor a breeze blow, without startling his repose,
64 and causing him to sally forth wrathfully from his den.

65 Though really a good-hearted, good-tempered old fellow at bottom, yet he is singularly
66 fond of being in the midst of contention. It is one of his peculiarities, however, that he only
67 relishes the beginning of an affray; he always goes into a fight with alacrity, but comes out
68 of it grumbling even when victorious; and though no one fights with more obstinacy to carry
69 a contested point, yet, when the battle is over, and he comes to the reconciliation, he is so
70 much taken up with the mere shaking of hands, that he is apt to let his antagonist pocket all
71 that they have been quarreling about. It is not, therefore, fighting that he ought so much to

72 be on his guard against, as making friends. It is difficult to cudgel him out of a farthing; but
73 put him in a good humor, and you may bargain him out of all the money in his pocket. He is
74 like a stout ship, which will weather the roughest storm uninjured, but roll its masts
75 overboard in the succeeding calm.

19. The character of John Bull is an example of:
    a. Allegory
    b. Personification
    c. Metaphor
    d. Figurative language

20. "He is like a stout ship, which will weather the roughest storm uninjured, but roll its masts overboard in the succeeding calm." is an example of:
    a. A simile
    b. A metaphor
    c. Personification
    d. Characterization

21. The author primarily uses:
    a. Abstract language
    b. Concrete language
    c. Figurative language
    d. Formal language

22. "Cudgeled" most nearly means:
    a. Saved
    b. Bludgeoned
    c. Scorned
    d. Beaten

23. The author's intent is to:
    a. Educate
    b. Inform
    c. Convince
    d. Entertain

24. "He excels in humor more than in wit; is jolly rather than gay; melancholy rather than morose; can easily be moved to a sudden tear, or surprised into a broad laugh; but he loathes sentiment, and has no turn for light pleasantry." This passage shows the use of:
    a. Paradoxes
    b. Oxymorons
    c. Anaphora
    d. Parallelism

25. "Couched in his little domain, with these filaments stretching forth in every direction, he is like some choleric, bottle-bellied old spider, who has woven his web over a whole chamber, so that a fly cannot buzz, nor a breeze blow, without startling his repose, and causing him to sally forth wrathfully from his den." This is an example of:
    a. Analogy
    b. Anecdote
    c. Allegory
    d. Assonance

26. The connotation of "broil" is:
    a. To cook under high heat
    b. A fight or argue
    c. To bring to a certain temperature
    d. Anger

27. The author does not use which of the following:
    a. Humor
    b. Irony
    c. Annotation
    d. Analogy

1   IT is natural to believe in great men. If the companions of our childhood should turn out to

2   be heroes, and their condition regal, it would not surprise us. All mythology opens with

3   demigods, and the circumstance is high and poetic; that is, their genius is paramount. In the

4   legends of the Gautama, the first men ate the earth, and found it deliciously sweet.

5   Nature seems to exist for the excellent. The world is upheld by the veracity of good men:

6   they make the earth wholesome. They who lived with them found life glad and nutritious.

7   Life is sweet and tolerable only in our belief in such society; and actually or ideally we

8   manage to live with superiors. We call our children and our lands by their names. Their

9   names are wrought into the verbs of language, their works and effigies are in our houses,

10   and every circumstance of the day recalls an anecdote of them.

11   The search after the great is the dream of youth and the most serious occupation of

12   manhood. We travel into foreign parts to find his works—if possible, to get a glimpse of

13   him. But we are put off with fortune instead. You say the English are practical; the Germans

14   are hospitable; in Valencia the climate is delicious; and in the hills of the Sacramento there

15   is gold for the gathering. Yes, but I do not travel to find comfortable, rich, and hospitable

16   people, or clear sky, or ingots that cost too much. But if there were any magnet that would

17   point to the countries and houses where are the persons who are intrinsically rich and

18   powerful, I would sell all, and buy it, and put myself on the road to-day.

19   The race goes with us on their credit. The knowledge that in the city is a man who invented

20   the railroad raises the credit of all the citizens. But enormous populations, if they be

21   beggars, are disgusting, like moving cheese, like hills of ants or of fleas—the more, the

22   worse.

23   Our religion is the love and cherishing of these patrons. The gods of fable are the shining

24   moments of great men. We run all our vessels into one mould. Our colossal theologies of

25   Judaism, Christism, Buddhism, Mahometism, are the necessary and structural action of the

26   human mind. The student of history is like a man going into a warehouse to buy cloths or

27   carpets. He fancies he has a new article. If he go to the factory, he shall find that his new

28   stuff still repeats the scrolls and rosettes which are found on the interior walls of the

29   pyramids of Thebes. Our theism is the purification of the human mind. Man can paint, or

30   make, or think nothing but man. He believes that the great material elements had their

31   origin from his thought. And our philosophy finds one essence collected or distributed.

32   If now we proceed to inquire into the kinds of service we derive from others, let us be

33   warned of the danger of modern studies, and begin low enough. We must not contend

34   against love, or deny the substantial existence of other people. I know not what would

35   happen to us. We have social strengths. Our affection towards others creates a sort of
36   vantage or purchase which nothing will supply. I can do that by another which I cannot do
37   alone. I can say to you what I cannot first say to myself. Other men are lenses through
38   which we read our own minds. Each man seeks those of different quality from his own, and
39   such as are good of their kind; that is, he seeks other men, and the *otherest*. The stronger
40   the nature, the more it is reactive. Let us have the quality pure. A little genius let us leave
41   alone. A main difference betwixt men is, whether they attend their own affair or not. Man is
42   that noble endogenous plant which grows, like the palm, from within outward. His own
43   affair, though impossible to others, he can open with celerity and in sport. It is easy to sugar
44   to be sweet, and to nitre to be salt. We take a great deal of pains to waylay and entrap that
45   which of itself will fall into our hands. I count him a great man who inhabits a higher sphere
46   of thought, into which other men rise with labor and difficulty; he has but to open his eyes
47   to see things in a true light, and in large relations; whilst they must make painful
48   corrections, and keep a vigilant eye on many sources of error. His service to us is of like sort.
49   It costs a beautiful person no exertion to paint her image on our eyes; yet how splendid is
50   that benefit! It costs no more for a wise soul to convey his quality to other men. And
51   everyone can do his best thing easiest. "*Peu de moyens, beaucoup d'effét.*" He is great who
52   is what he is from nature, and who never reminds us of others.

28. Which of the following is the earth and nature compared to?
    a. Humanity
    b. Food
    c. Sports
    d. Art

29. The following line, "The student of history is like a man going into a warehouse to buy cloths or carpets," may be considered to be all of the following:
    a. Analogy, metaphor, simile
    b. Analogy, simile, figurative language
    c. Concrete language, simile, personification
    d. Simile, abstract language, figurative language

30. The main idea of this passage is:
    a. We admire great men.
    b. Great men have made the world better.
    c. Improvements come because we seek greatness.
    d. Greatness is natural, not contrived.

31. In this text, greatness is primarily identified as:
    a. A spiritual condition
    b. Intellectual ability
    c. Wealth and power
    d. Service to others

32. The author connects religion to:
    a. The supernatural
    b. The search for knowledge
    c. Greatness
    d. Wealth

33. Which of the following may represent a contradiction in the author's work?
    a. He identifies both spiritual and worldly leaders as great.
    b. Wealth is not necessarily a sign of greatness.
    c. The great are not demi-gods
    d. The large numbers of the poor suggest misery, not greatness.

34. The author is guilty of a rhetorical fallacy. Which rhetorical fallacy appears in this passage?
    a. An ad hominem argument
    b. Begging the question
    c. Argument from ignorance
    d. Appeal to false authority

35. The author's language in this passage is largely:
    a. Concrete
    b. Figurative
    c. Abstract
    d. Colloquial

Oliver Wendell Holmes. Bread and the Newspaper.

1   THIS is the new version of the *Panem et Circenses* of the Roman populace. It is our
2   *ultimatum*, as that was theirs. They must have something to eat, and the circus-shows to
3   look at. We must have something to eat, and the papers to read.

4   Everything else we can give up. If we are rich, we can lay down our carriages, stay away
5   from Newport or Saratoga, and adjourn the trip to Europe *sine die*. If we live in a small way,
6   there are at least new dresses and bonnets and every-day luxuries which we can dispense
7   with. If the young Zouave of the family looks smart in his new uniform, its respectable head
8   is content, though he himself grow seedy as a caraway-umbel late in the season. He will
9   cheerfully calm the perturbed nap of his old beaver by patient brushing in place of buying a
10 new one, if only the Lieutenant's jaunty cap is what it should be. We all take a pride in
11 sharing the epidemic economy of the time. Only *bread and the newspaper* we must have,
12 whatever else we do without.

13 How this war is simplifying our mode of being! We live on our emotions, as the sick man is
14 said in the common speech to be nourished by his fever. Our ordinary mental food has
15 become distasteful, and what would have been intellectual luxuries at other times, are now
16 absolutely repulsive.

17 All this change in our manner of existence implies that we have experienced some very
18 profound impression, which will sooner or later betray itself in permanent effects on the
19 minds and bodies of many among us. We cannot forget Corvisart's observation of the
20 frequency with which diseases of the heart were noticed as the consequence of the terrible
21 emotions produced by the scenes of the great French Revolution. Laennec tells the story of
22 a convent, of which he was the medical director, where all the nuns were subjected to the
23 severest penances and schooled in the most painful doctrines. They all became
24 consumptive soon after their entrance, so that, in the course of his ten years' attendance,
25 all the inmates died out two or three times, and were replaced by new ones. He does not
26 hesitate to attribute the disease from which they suffered to those depressing moral
27 influences to which they were subjected.

28 So far we have noticed little more than disturbances of the nervous system as a
29 consequence of the war excitement in non-combatants. Take the first trifling example
30 which comes to our recollection. A sad disaster to the Federal army was told the other day
31 in the presence of two gentlemen and a lady. Both the gentlemen complained of a sudden
32 feeling at the *epigastrium*, or, less learnedly, the pit of the stomach, changed color, and
33 confessed to a slight tremor about the knees. The lady had a "*grande révolution*," as French
34 patients say,—went home, and kept her bed for the rest of the day. Perhaps the reader may
35 smile at the mention of such trivial indispositions, but in more sensitive natures death itself

36   follows in some cases from no more serious cause. An old gentleman fell senseless in fatal
37   apoplexy, on hearing of Napoleon's return from Elba. One of our early friends, who recently
38   died of the same complaint, was thought to have had his attack mainly in consequence of
39   the excitements of the time.

40   We all know what the *war fever* is in our young men,—what a devouring passion it becomes
41   in those whom it assails. Patriotism is the fire of it, no doubt, but this is fed with fuel of all
42   sorts. The love of adventure, the contagion of example, the fear of losing the chance of
43   participating in the great events of the time, the desire of personal distinction, all help to
44   produce those singular transformations which we often witness, turning the most peaceful
45   of our youth into the most ardent of our soldiers. But something of the same fever in a
46   different form reaches a good many non-combatants, who have no thought of losing a drop
47   of precious blood belonging to themselves or their families. Some of the symptoms we shall
48   mention are almost universal; they are as plain in the people we meet everywhere as the
49   marks of an influenza, when that is prevailing.

50   The first is a nervous restlessness of a very peculiar character. Men cannot think, or write,
51   or attend to their ordinary business. They stroll up and down the streets, or saunter out
52   upon the public places. We confessed to an illustrious author that we laid down the volume
53   of his work which we were reading when the war broke out. It was as interesting as a
54   romance, but the romance of the past grew pale before the red light of the terrible present.
55   Meeting the same author not long afterwards, he confessed that he had laid down his pen
56   at the same time that we had closed his book. He could not write about the sixteenth
57   century any more than we could read about it, while the nineteenth was in the very agony
58   and bloody sweat of its great sacrifice.

59   Another most eminent scholar told us in all simplicity that he had fallen into such a state
60   that he would read the same telegraphic dispatches over and over again in different papers,
61   as if they were new, until he felt as if he were an idiot. Who did not do just the same thing,
62   and does not often do it still, now that the first flush of the fever is over? Another person
63   always goes through the side streets on his way for the noon *extra*,—he is so afraid
64   somebody will meet him and *tell* the news he wishes to *read*, first on the bulletin-board,
65   and then in the great capitals and leaded type of the newspaper.

66   When any startling piece of war-news comes, it keeps repeating itself in our minds in spite
67   of all we can do. The same trains of thought go tramping round in circle through the brain,
68   like the supernumeraries that make up the grand army of a stage-show. Now, if a thought
69   goes round through the brain a thousand times in a day, it will have worn as deep a track as
70   one which has passed through it once a week for twenty years. This accounts for the ages
71   we seem to have lived since the twelfth of April last, and, to state it more generally, for that

72   *ex post facto* operation of a great calamity, or any very powerful impression, which we once

73   illustrated by the image of a stain spreading backwards from the leaf of life open before us

74   through all those which we have already turned.

75   Blessed are those who can sleep quietly in times like these! Yet, not wholly blessed, either:

76   for what is more painful than the awaking from peaceful unconsciousness to a sense that

77   there is something wrong,—we cannot at first think what,—and then groping our way about

78   through the twilight of our thoughts until we come full upon the misery, which, like some

79   evil bird, seemed to have flown away, but which sits waiting for us on its perch by our pillow

80   in the gray of the morning?

36. Why has the newspaper become so critical?
    a. Literacy rates have improved.
    b. The country is at war.
    c. There is famine.
    d. It is the only way to get news.

37. "The same trains of thought go tramping round in circle through the brain, like the supernumeraries that make up the grand army of a stage-show," is an example of:
    a. An analogy
    b. An argument
    c. An allegory
    d. A paradox

38. The author believes that the need for newspapers is?
    a. Emotional
    b. Logical
    c. Irrational
    d. Unconscious

39. The author contrasts the newspaper and:
    a. Television
    b. Radio
    c. Novels
    d. Circuses

40. To what does "ordinary mental food" refer?
    a. Newspapers
    b. Novels and other entertainment
    c. Conversation
    d. War

41. The following, "nineteenth was in the very agony and bloody sweat of its great sacrifice" is an example what rhetorical device?
    a. Personification
    b. Cacophony
    c. Alliteration
    d. Sarcasm

42. In "Now, if a thought goes round through the brain a thousand times in a day, it will have worn as deep a track as one which has passed through it once a week for twenty years." what is the antecedent for "it"?
    a. The war
    b. The thought
    c. The train
    d. The track

43. "Yet, not wholly blessed, either: for what is more painful than the awaking from peaceful unconsciousness to a sense that there is something wrong,—we cannot at first think what,—and then groping our way about through the twilight of our thoughts until we come full upon the misery, which, like some evil bird, seemed to have flown away, but which sits waiting for us on its perch by our pillow in the gray of the morning?" is an example of what?
    a. Appeal to the bandwagon
    b. Complex sentence
    c. Parallelism
    d. Rhetorical question

44. Which of the following is an example of an anecdote?
    a. "We confessed to an illustrious author that we laid down the volume of his work which we were reading when the war broke out. It was as interesting as a romance, but the romance of the past grew pale before the red light of the terrible present. Meeting the same author not long afterwards, he confessed that he had laid down his pen at the same time that we had closed his book."
    b. "Blessed are those who can sleep quietly in times like these!"
    c. "The first is a nervous restlessness of a very peculiar character."
    d. "THIS is the new version of the *Panem et Circenses* of the Roman populace."

45. " The love of adventure, the contagion of example, the fear of losing the chance of participating in the great events of the time, the desire of personal distinction, all help to produce those singular transformations which we often witness, turning the most peaceful of our youth into the most ardent of our soldiers." is an example of a:
    a. Complex sentence
    b. Cumulative sentence
    c. Periodic sentence
    d. Compound sentence

1 I have met with but one or two persons in the course of my life who understood the art of
2 Walking, that is, of taking walks,—who had a genius, so to speak, for *sauntering*: which
3 word is beautifully derived from "idle people who roved about the country, in the Middle
4 Ages, and asked charity, under pretense of going *à la Sainte Terre*," to the Holy Land, till the
5 children exclaimed, "There goes a *Sainte-Terrer*," a Saunterer,—a Holy-Lander. They who
6 never go to the Holy Land in their walks, as they pretend, are indeed mere idlers and
7 vagabonds; but they who do go there are saunterers in the good sense, such as I mean.
8 Some, however, would derive the word from *sans terre*, without land or a home, which,
9 therefore, in the good sense, will mean, having no particular home, but equally at home
10 everywhere. For this is the secret of successful sauntering. He who sits still in a house all the
11 time may be the greatest vagrant of all; but the saunterer, in the good sense, is no more
12 vagrant than the meandering river, which is all the while sedulously seeking the shortest
13 course to the sea. But I prefer the first, which, indeed, is the most probable derivation. For
14 every walk is a sort of crusade, preached by some Peter the Hermit in us, to go forth and
15 reconquer this Holy Land from the hands of the Infidels.

16 It is true, we are but faint-hearted crusaders, even the walkers, nowadays, who undertake
17 no persevering, never-ending enterprises. Our expeditions are but tours, and come round
18 again at evening to the old hearth-side from which we set out. Half the walk is but retracing
19 our steps. We should go forth on the shortest walk, perchance, in the spirit of undying
20 adventure, never to return,—prepared to send back our embalmed hearts only as relics to
21 our desolate kingdoms. If you are ready to leave father and mother, and brother and sister,
22 and wife and child and friends, and never see them again,—if you have paid your debts, and
23 made your will, and settled all your affairs, and are a free man, then you are ready for a
24 walk.

25 To come down to my own experience, my companion and I, for I sometimes have a
26 companion, take pleasure in fancying ourselves knights of a new, or rather an old, order,—
27 not Equestrians or Chevaliers, not Ritters or riders, but Walkers, a still more ancient and
28 honorable class, I trust. The chivalric and heroic spirit which once belonged to the Rider
29 seems now to reside in, or perchance to have subsided into, the Walker,—not the Knight,
30 but Walker Errant. He is a sort of fourth estate, outside of Church and State and People.

31 We have felt that we almost alone hereabouts practiced this noble art; though, to tell the
32 truth, at least, if their own assertions are to be received, most of my townsmen would fain
33 walk sometimes, as I do, but they cannot. No wealth can buy the requisite leisure, freedom,
34 and independence, which are the capital in this profession. It comes only by the grace of
35 God. It requires a direct dispensation from Heaven to become a walker. You must be born

into the family of the Walkers. *Ambulator nascitur, non fit.* Some of my townsmen, it is true, can remember and have described to me some walks which they took ten years ago, in which they were so blessed as to lose themselves for half an hour in the woods; but I know very well that they have confined themselves to the highway ever since, whatever pretensions they may make to belong to this select class. No doubt they were elevated for a moment as by the reminiscence of a previous state of existence, when even they were foresters and outlaws.

> "When he came to grene wode,
>
> In a mery mornynge,
>
> There he herde the notes small
>
> Of byrdes mery syngynge.
>
> "It is ferre gone, sayd Robyn,
>
> That I was last here;
>
> Me lyste a lytell for to shote
>
> At the donne dere."

I think that I cannot preserve my health and spirits, unless I spend four hours a day at least,—and it is commonly more than that,—sauntering through the woods and over the hills and fields, absolutely free from all worldly engagements. You may safely say, A penny for your thoughts, or a thousand pounds. When sometimes I am reminded that the mechanics and shopkeepers stay in their shops not only all the forenoon, but all the afternoon too, sitting with crossed legs, so many of them,—as if the legs were made to sit upon, and not to stand or walk upon,—I think that they deserve some credit for not having all committed suicide long ago.

I, who cannot stay in my chamber for a single day without acquiring some rust, and when sometimes I have stolen forth for a walk at the eleventh hour of four o'clock in the afternoon, too late to redeem the day, when the shades of night were already beginning to be mingled with the daylight, have felt as if I had committed some sin to be atoned for,—I confess that I am astonished at the power of endurance, to say nothing of the moral insensibility, of my neighbors who confine themselves to shops and offices the whole day for weeks and months, ay, and years almost together. I know not what manner of stuff they are of,—sitting there now at three o'clock in the afternoon, as if it were three o'clock in the morning. Bonaparte may talk of the three-o'clock-in-the-morning courage, but it is nothing to the courage which can sit down cheerfully at this hour in the afternoon over against one's self whom you have known all the morning, to starve out a garrison to whom you are

70 bound by such strong ties of sympathy. I wonder that about this time, or say between four
71 and five o'clock in the afternoon, too late for the morning papers and too early for the
72 evening ones, there is not a general explosion heard up and down the street, scattering a
73 legion of antiquated and house-bred notions and whims to the four winds for an airing,—
74 and so the evil cure itself.

1

46. The author compares a walk to a crusade. This is an example of:
   a. An anecdote
   b. Analogy
   c. Onomatopoeia
   d. Alliteration

47. In "Bonaparte may talk of the three-o'clock-in-the-morning courage, but it is nothing
    to the courage which can sit down cheerfully at this hour in the afternoon over
    against one's self whom you have known all the morning, to starve out a garrison to
    whom you are bound by such strong ties of sympathy." "it" refers to what
    antecedent?
   a. Bonaparte
   b. This hour
   c. Three-o'clock-in-the-morning courage
   d. Walking

48. "As the marks of an influenza" is an example of:
   a. A metaphor
   b. Abstract language
   c. A motif
   d. A simile

49. "A penny for your thoughts, or a thousand pounds." is an:
   a. Analogy
   b. Aphorism
   c. Cliche
   d. Metaphor

50. The author's tone is:
    a. Romantic
    b. Sober
    c. Fearful
    d. Cheerful

51. This piece is an example of what type of writing?
    a. Expository
    b. Narrative
    c. Persuasive
    d. Argumentative

52. What is required to be a walker?
    a. Wealth
    b. Physical ability and time
    c. Leisure and wealth
    d. Leisure, freedom and independence

53. What does "saunterer" mean?
    a. Vagrant
    b. Holy-Lander
    c. Idler
    d. Crusader

54. The author believes that the value of walking is found in:
    a. Exercise
    b. The opportunity to see new things
    c. Not spending time in an office
    d. Spending time in nature

55. "For every walk is a sort of crusade, preached by some Peter the Hermit in us, to go forth and reconquer this Holy Land from the hands of the Infidels." is an example of:
    a. An analogy
    b. An anecdote
    c. An allusion
    d. Classicism

From Henry Cabot Lodge's Colonialism in the United States. Read this passage and write an essay explaining how Lodge used language and rhetoric in his writing.

In the year of grace 1776, we published to the world our Declaration of Independence. Six years later, England assented to the separation. These are tolerably familiar facts. That we have been striving ever since to make that independence real and complete, and that the work is not yet entirely finished, are not, perhaps, equally obvious truisms. The hard fighting by which we severed our connection with the mother-country was in many ways the least difficult part of the work of building up a great and independent nation. The decision of the sword may be rude, but it is pretty sure to be speedy. Armed revolution is quick. A South American, in the exercise of his constitutional privileges, will rush into the street and declare a revolution in five minutes. A Frenchman will pull down one government to-day, and set up another to-morrow, besides giving new names to all the principal streets of Paris during the intervening night. We English-speaking people do not move quite so fast. We come more slowly to the boiling point; we are not fond of violent changes, and when we make them we consume a considerable time in the operation. Still, at the best, a revolution by force of arms is an affair of a few years. We broke with England in 1776, we had won our victory in 1782, and by the year 1789 we had a new national government fairly started.

But if we are slower than other people in the conduct of revolutions, owing largely to our love of dogged fighting and inability to recognize defeat, we are infinitely more deliberate than our neighbors in altering, or even modifying, our ideas and modes of thought. The slow mind and ingrained conservatism of the English race are the chief causes of their marvelous political and material success. After much obstinate fighting in the field, they have carried through the few revolutions which they have seen fit to engage in; but when they have undertaken to extend these revolutions to the domain of thought, there has arisen a spirit of stubborn and elusive resistance, which has seemed to set every effort, and even time itself, at defiance.

By the treaty of Paris our independence was acknowledged, and in name and theory was complete. We then entered upon the second stage in the conflict, that of ideas and opinions. True to our race and to our instincts, and with a wisdom which is one of the glories of our history, we carefully preserved the principles and forms of government and law, which traced an unbroken descent and growth from the days of the Saxon invasion. But while we kept so much that was of inestimable worth, we also retained, inevitably, of course, something which it would have been well for us to have shaken off together with the rule of George III. and the British Parliament. This was the colonial spirit in our modes of thought.

The word "colonial" is preferable to the more obvious word "provincial," because the former is absolute, while the latter, by usage, has become in a great measure relative. We are very apt to call an opinion, a custom, or a neighbor "provincial," because we do not like the person or thing in question; and in this way the true value of the word has of late been frittered away. "Colonialism," moreover, has in this connection historical point and value, while "provincialism" is general and meaningless. Colonialism is also susceptible of accurate definition. A colony is an off-shoot from a parent stock, and its chief characteristic is dependence. In exact proportion as dependence lessens, the colony changes its nature and advances toward national existence. For a hundred and fifty years we were English colonies. Just before the revolution, in everything but the affairs of practical government, the precise point at which the break came, we were still colonies in the fullest sense of the term. Except in matters of food and drink, and of the wealth which we won from the soil and the ocean, we were in a state of complete material and intellectual dependence. Every luxury, and almost every manufactured article, came to us across the water. Our politics, except those which were purely local, were the politics of England, and so also were our foreign relations. Our books, our art, our authors, our commerce, were all English; and this was true of our colleges, our professions, our learning, our fashions, and our manners. There is no need here to go into the details which show the absolute supremacy of the colonial spirit and our entire intellectual dependence. When we sought to originate, we simply imitated. The conditions of our life could not be overcome.

This short excerpt, taken from Edward Sandford Martin's The Tyranny of Things discusses the writer's perception of needs, wealth and modernization. Your argumentative essay should refute, support or qualify this text and his interpretations.

A TRAVELER newly returned from the Pacific Ocean tells pleasant stories of the Patagonians. As the steamer he was in was passing through Magellan's Straits some natives came out to her in boats. They wore no clothes at all, though there was snow in the air. A baby that came along with them made some demonstration that displeased its mother, who took it by the foot, as Thetis took Achilles, and soused it over the side of the boat into the cold seawater. When she pulled it in, it lay a moment whimpering in the bottom of the boat, and then curled up and went to sleep. The missionaries there have tried to teach the natives to wear clothes, and to sleep in huts; but, so far, the traveler says, with very limited success. The most shelter a Patagonian can endure is a little heap of rocks or a log to the windward of him; as for clothes, he despises them, and he is indifferent to ornament.

To many of us, groaning under the oppression of modern conveniences, it seems lamentably meddlesome to undermine the simplicity of such people, and enervate them with the luxuries of civilization. To be able to sleep out-o-doors, and go naked, and take sea-baths on wintry days with impunity, would seem a most alluring emancipation. No rent to pay, no tailor, no plumber, no newspaper to be read on pain of getting behind the times; no regularity in anything, not even meals; nothing to do except to find food, and no expense for undertakers or physicians, even if we fail; what a fine, untrammeled life it would be! It takes occasional contact with such people as the Patagonians to keep us in mind that civilization is the mere cultivation of our wants, and that the higher it is the more our necessities are multiplied, until, if we are rich enough, we get enervated by luxury, and the young men come in and carry us out.

We want so many, many things, it seems a pity that those simple Patagonians could not send missionaries to us to show us how to do without. The comforts of life, at the rate they are increasing, bid fair to bury us soon, as Tarpeia was buried under the shields of her friends the Sabines. Mr. Hamerton, in speaking of the increase of comfort in England, groans at the "trying strain of expense to which our extremely high standard of living subjects all except the rich." It makes each individual of us very costly to keep, and constantly tempts people to concentrate on the maintenance of fewer individuals means that would in simpler times be divided among many. "My grandfather," said a modern the other day, "left $200,000. He was considered a rich man in those days; but, dear me! he supported four or five families—all his needy relations and all my grandmother's." Think of an income of $10,000 a year being equal to such a strain, and providing suitably for a rich man's large family in the bargain! It wouldn't go so far now, and yet most of the reasonable necessaries of life cost less to-day than they did two generations ago. The difference is that we need so very many comforts that were not invented in our grandfather's time.

There is a hospital, in a city large enough to keep a large hospital busy, that is in straits for money. Its income from contributions last year was larger by nearly a third than its income ten years ago, but its expenses were nearly double its income. There were some satisfactory reasons for the discrepancy—the city had grown, the number of patients had increased, extraordinary repairs had been made—but at the bottom a very large expenditure seemed to be due to the struggle of the managers to keep the institution up to modern standards. The patients are better cared for than they used to be; the nurses are better taught and more skillful; "conveniences" have been greatly multiplied; the heating and cooking and laundry work is all done in the best manner with the most approved apparatus; the plumbing is as safe as sanitary engineering can make it; the appliances for antiseptic surgery are fit for a fight for life; there are detached buildings for contagious diseases, and an out-patient department, and the whole concern is administered with wisdom and economy. There is only one distressing circumstance about this excellent charity, and that is that its expenses exceed its income. And yet its managers have not been extravagant: they have only done what the enlightened experience of the day has considered to be necessary. If the hospital has to shut down and the patients must be turned out, at least the receiver will find a well-appointed institution of which the managers have no reason to be ashamed.

The trouble seems to be with very many of us, in contemporary private life as well as in institutions, that the enlightened experience of the day invents more necessaries than we can get the money to pay for. Our opulent friends are constantly demonstrating to us by example how indispensably convenient the modern necessaries are, and we keep having them until we either exceed our incomes or miss the higher concerns of life in the effort to maintain a complete outfit of its creature comforts.

Use two or more of these sources, all dealing with the actions of the Nazi Party during World War II, in an essay on the subject. Synthesize the material in these sources to produce your own analysis.

Cardinal Clemens von Galen. Against Nazi Euthanasia.

However, there are sacred obligations of conscience from which no one has the power to release us and which we must fulfil even if it costs us our lives. Never under any circumstances may a human being kill an innocent person apart from war and legitimate self-defense. On July 6, I already had cause to add to the pastoral letter the following explanation: for some months we have been hearing reports that, on the orders of Berlin, patients from mental asylums who have been ill for a long time and may appear incurable, are being compulsorily removed. Then, after a short time, the relatives are regularly informed that the corpse has been burnt and the ashes can be delivered. There is a general suspicion verging on certainty, that these numerous unexpected deaths of mentally ill people do not occur of themselves but are deliberately brought about, that the doctrine is being followed, according to which one may destroy so-called 'worthless life,' that is, kill innocent people if one considers that their lives are of no further value for the nation and the state.

I am reliably informed that lists are also being drawn up in the asylums of the province of Westphalia as well of those patients who are to be taken away as so-called 'unproductive national comrades' and shortly to be killed. The first transport left the Marienthal institution near Münster during this past week.

German men and women, section 211 of the Reich Penal Code is still valid. It states: 'He who deliberately kills another person will be punished by death for murder if the killing is premeditated.'

Those patients who are destined to be killed are transported away from home to a distant asylum presumably in order to protect those who deliberately kill those poor people, members of our families, from this legal punishment. Some illness is then given as the cause of death. Since the corpse has been burnt straight away, the relatives and also the criminal police are unable to establish whether the illness really occurred and what the cause of death was.

However, I have been assured that the Reich Interior Ministry and the office of the Reich Doctors' Leader, Dr. Conti, make no bones about the fact that in reality a large number of mentally ill people in Germany have been deliberately killed and more will be killed in the future.

The Penal Code lays down in section 139: 'He who receives credible information concerning the intention to commit a crime against life and neglects to alert the authorities or the person who is threatened in time...will be punished.'

When I learned of the intention to transport patients from Marienthal in order to kill them, I brought a formal charge at the State Court in Münster and with the Police President in Münster by means of a registered letter which read as follows: "According to information which I have received, in the course of this week a large number of patients from the Marienthal Provincial Asylum near Münster are to be transported to the Eichberg asylum as so-called 'unproductive national comrades' and will then soon be deliberately killed, as is generally believed has occurred with such transports from other asylums. Since such an action is not only contrary to the moral laws of God and Nature but also is punishable with death as murder under section 211 of the Penal Code, I hereby bring a charge in accordance with my duty under section 139 of the Penal Code, and request you to provide immediate protection for the national comrades threatened in this way by taking action against those agencies who are intending their removal and murder, and that you inform me of the steps that have been taken."

I have received no news concerning intervention by the Prosecutor's Office or by the police...Thus we must assume that the poor helpless patients will soon be killed.

For what reason?

Not because they have committed a crime worthy of death. Not because they attacked their nurses or orderlies so that the latter had no other choice but to use legitimate force to defend their lives against their attackers. Those are cases where, in addition to the killing of an armed enemy in a just war, the use of force to the point of killing is allowed and is often required.

No, it is not for such reasons that these unfortunate patients must die but rather because, in the opinion of some department, on the testimony of some commission, they have become 'worthless life' because according to this testimony they are 'unproductive national comrades.' The argument goes: they can no longer produce commodities, they are like an old machine that no longer works, they are like an old horse which has become incurably lame, they are like a cow which no longer gives milk.

What does one do with such an old machine? It is thrown on the scrap heap. What does one do with a lame horse, with such an unproductive cow?

Edouard Daladier. The Nazis' Aim is Slavery.

The domination at which the Nazis aim is not limited to the displacement of the balance of power and the imposition of supremacy of one nation. It seeks the systematic and total destruction of those conquered by Hitler, and it does not treaty with the nations which he has subdued. He destroys them. He takes from them their whole political and economic existence and seeks even to deprive them of their history and their culture. He wishes to consider them only as vital space and a vacant territory over which he has every right.

The human beings who constitute these nations are for him only cattle. He orders their massacre or their migration. He compels them to make room for their conquerors. He does not even take the trouble to impose any war tribute on them. He just takes all their wealth, and, to prevent any revolt, he wipes out their leaders and scientifically seeks the physical and moral degradation of those whose independence he has taken away.

Under this domination, in thousands of towns and villages in Europe there are millions of human beings now living in misery which, some months ago, they could never have imagined. Austria, Bohemia, Slovakia and Poland are only lands of despair. Their whole peoples have been deprived of the means of moral and material happiness. Subdued by treachery or brutal violence, they have no other recourse than to work for their executioners who grant them scarcely enough to assure the most miserable existence.

There is being created a world of masters and slaves in the image of Germany herself. For, while Germany is crushing beneath her tyranny the men of every race and language, she is herself being crushed beneath her own servitude and her domination mania. The German worker and peasant are the slaves of their Nazi masters while the worker and peasant of Bohemia and Poland have become in turn slaves of these slaves. Before this first realization of a mad dream, the whole world might shudder.

Elie Wiesel. The Perils of Indifference.

What is indifference? Etymologically, the word means "no difference." A strange and unnatural state in which the lines blur between light and darkness, dusk and dawn, crime and punishment, cruelty and compassion, good and evil.

What are its courses and inescapable consequences? Is it a philosophy? Is there a philosophy of indifference conceivable? Can one possibly view indifference as a virtue? Is it necessary at times to practice it simply to keep one's sanity, live normally, enjoy a fine meal and a glass of wine, as the world around us experiences harrowing upheavals?

Of course, indifference can be tempting -- more than that, seductive. It is so much easier to look away from victims. It is so much easier to avoid such rude interruptions to our work, our dreams, our hopes. It is, after all, awkward, troublesome, to be involved in another person's pain and despair. Yet, for the person who is indifferent, his or her neighbor are of no consequence. And, therefore, their lives are meaningless. Their hidden or even visible anguish is of no interest. Indifference reduces the other to an abstraction.

Over there, behind the black gates of Auschwitz, the most tragic of all prisoners were the "Muselmanner," as they were called. Wrapped in their torn blankets, they would sit or lie on the ground, staring vacantly into space, unaware of who or where they were, strangers to their surroundings. They no longer felt pain, hunger, thirst. They feared nothing. They felt nothing. They were dead and did not know it.

Rooted in our tradition, some of us felt that to be abandoned by humanity then was not the ultimate. We felt that to be abandoned by God was worse than to be punished by Him. Better an unjust God than an indifferent one. For us to be ignored by God was a harsher punishment than to be a victim of His anger. Man can live far from God -- not outside God. God is wherever we are. Even in suffering? Even in suffering.

In a way, to be indifferent to that suffering is what makes the human being inhuman. Indifference, after all, is more dangerous than anger and hatred. Anger can at times be creative. One writes a great poem, a great symphony, one does something special for the sake of humanity because one is angry at the injustice that one witnesses. But indifference is never creative. Even hatred at times may elicit a response. You fight it. You denounce it. You disarm it. Indifference elicits no response. Indifference is not a response.

Indifference is not a beginning, it is an end. And, therefore, indifference is always the friend of the enemy, for it benefits the aggressor -- never his victim, whose pain is magnified when he or she feels forgotten. The political prisoner in his cell, the hungry children, the homeless refugees -- not to respond to their plight, not to relieve their solitude by offering them a spark of hope is to exile them from human memory. And in denying their humanity we betray our own.

Indifference, then, is not only a sin, it is a punishment. And this is one of the most important lessons of this outgoing century's wide-ranging experiments in good and evil.

Martin Niemoller.

First they came for the Socialists, and I did not speak out--
Because I was not a Socialist.

Then they came for the Trade Unionists, and I did not speak out--
Because I was not a Trade Unionist.

Then they came for the Jews, and I did not speak out--
Because I was not a Jew.

Then they came for me--and there was no one left to speak for me.

Practice Test 3 Answer Key

1. d	2. a	3. c	4. b	5. a	6. c	7. c
8. c	9. b	10. a	11. b	12. c	13. a	14. a
15. c	16. a	17. b	18. b	19. a	20. a	21. c
22. d	23. d	24. d	25. b	26. a	27. c	28. a
29. b	30. d	31. c	32. c	33. a	34. b	35. b
36. b	37. a	38. a	39. d	40. b	41. a	42. b
43. d	44. a	45. c	46. b	47. c	48. d	49. c
50. a	51. c	52. d	53. b	54. d	55. c	

Expository Essay 3

Henry Cabot Lodge's On Colonialism in the United States is a relatively straightforward exposition on the subject of the formation of the United States and the development of the young nation. He relies upon comparisons to other nations, as well as the presentation of facts, easily verified. His writing style is familiar and accessible, enabling the reader to connect with him as a writer and with his expository essay.

He begins this passage with a discussion of relatively common and well-known facts, including the basic dates of the American Revolution. He refers to these as "tolerably well known". While the reader of such an essay is likely well aware of these dates, their inclusion helps to engage the reader. These dates also add provide the writer with authority. His work is, from early in this passage, supported by factual evidence. The first paragraph concludes much as it began, with dates and facts, basic incontrovertible evidence. This is an argument based on ethos, rather than pathos.

Lodge places the basic facts of the American Revolution within a broader international context, comparing the American Revolution to other well-known revolutions. He refers to the quick conflicts common in France and South America. In these countries, revolution happens nearly instantaneously. While his suggestion that street names were changed during the night may be hyperbole, he successfully illustrates the difference between the American Revolution and others, like the French Revolution. These revolutions and changes were harsh and violent, but quickly achieved. The American Revolution took longer, was slower in coming, and was followed by the languid development of a new government.

Once the context is established, Lodge focuses on the character of the nation. Americans, like the English, are, according to Lodge, deliberate. He suggests that this aspect of the American character comes from the English, again offering up historical and factual precedents, including, in this case, the Saxon invasion. In this, we find the reference to the title of this essay. He questions the colonialism or provincialism of the American culture, explaining the connotations of the words he uses in some detail. While the author clearly values the deliberation of the founding fathers, he questions the reliance upon English customs, goods, and thought. Lodge appears to want a new, wholly American culture, free from the strong influence of the English.

While some authors rely upon figurative language and imagery to invoke emotion in their readers, Henry Cabot Lodge opts for simplicity, facts, and logic. He presents himself as an authority figure, supporting his argument with recognizable facts. His facts and comparisons create a context, even as he moves, eventually, to the presentation of new ideas for analysis and exposition.

201

Argumentative Essay 3

Edward Sandford Martin argues that we would be better off, happier, more content without modern conveniences and necessities. Martin's essay is relatively limited in his perspective, as he ignores possible benefits to modern technology and conveniences. He idealizes a simple life, creating an argument that is, in itself, overly simplistic. Oversimplification is a rhetorical fallacy, weakening this essay. His argument is largely, but not entirely emotional, as he includes a discussion of facts and figures in support of it. While he may support his argument, it is, from the beginning of the essay, a failed one.

Martin begins his essay from a place of privilege. He recounts the experiences of travelers on a steamboat, presumably white and wealthy, to Patagonia. There, they encounter people who live without clothing and shelter, without money, and, in Martin's mind, without worries. They have no material goods, no modern conveniences. The observers are clearly the very opposite of the Patagonians, viewing them from the decks of a luxurious steamboat. Martin says that he has heard of the Patagonians from one such traveler. In this, he begins an argument that fails. There is little of value in hearsay.

After a brief introduction to the Patagonians, he proceeds from what is, fundamentally, his conclusion. He is begging the question. The conclusion of his argument is a working assumption that his reader agrees that a state without wealth or material goods is better than the alternative. According to Martin, these conveniences are "lamentably meddlesome". Those modern traits so guilty of being meddlesome appear to include jobs, information, education, clothing and housing. The modern reader, and even, presumably, many 19th century readers, cannot help but find little appealing in a life without basic necessities, like clothing and shelter.

Martin moves on to a discussion of the financial challenges caused by modern living. He cites, as a factual example, the finances of a hospital. While the hospital is bringing in larger donations, additional costs, for such things as hygiene and laundry, have left the hospital lacking necessary funds. Of course, the hospital has also been faced with a larger population and additional patients. Even the most surface examination of Martin's example suggests that it is fallacious. His own facts are contradictory. Modern technology is responsible for these costs, but the hospital serves a larger population. A larger population, alone, would increase hospital costs. He does not consider possible benefits to new technological innovations, including those that might reduce significant problems, like infection.

While Martin may celebrate the simple life, he does so poorly. The central thesis of his argument may be valid, as yes, adding additional goods and needs to daily life does add costs and may provide little satisfaction. Even though his thesis may be defensible, Martin defends it poorly. His examples are ineffective and his argument poorly constructed.

Synthesis Essay 3

While the responsibility for the horrors of the Holocaust rests on the shoulders of those who perpetrated the crimes, they were able to commit atrocities because of the fundamental indifference of many Germans during the early years of the Nazi party, well before the implementation of Aktion T-4 and the so-called Final Solution. Those who spoke out in Germany, like the Cardinal, were rare and were often punished. Outside of Germany, little was said until countries, like France, were at risk themselves. While Niemoller's quote postdates the war, it is representative of the conditions in Germany. Each group remained quiet, because they were not, themselves, in danger. This is historical fact, but how did the few protest and speak out amidst this very indifference?

Cardinal Clemons von Galen learned of the Nazi euthanasia program and, moved by his moral conscience, spoke out from the pulpit. In doing so, he risked his own health and well-being, as well as his very life. His speech was not just from a single pulpit, but distributed to churches throughout Germany. The Cardinal's argument is emotional, logical and authoritative. He cites the moral authority of the Church, but also calls upon the personal connections individuals may have to the sick, the mentally ill and the disabled. His figurative language does not romanticize the situation, but rather forces the listener to recognize the very ugliness and horror of it.

The French prime minister spoke out against the horrors of the Nazis following the invasion of Poland, but before France itself was invaded. He was prepared for war, rather than indifferent, but he would not be successful in his fight against the Nazis. His use of figurative language, like that of the Cardinal, is intended to bring the horror of the war to life, with vivid imagery. The people, specifically those in Poland, are compared to cattle. While he may have spoken out, he did so once it was already too late. Perhaps, as the Nazi party rose to power, other countries, like France, could have taken action to change the political fates of Germany. They did not speak then, because the Germans did not come for them.

These speeches are impassioned and horrified, but they bring with them an air of hopelessness. The Cardinal's speech did little but cause the Nazis to work a bit harder to hide the killings of disabled children and the mentally ill. The French fell to the Nazis, regardless of resistance efforts. Niemoller spent his life, after he was released from the Dachau concentration camp, trying to alleviate his own guilt over his indifference. Even for those who tried, this was a battle that required the attention, the efforts and the struggle of the many. When the many are indifferent, the few have little impact.

Holocaust survivor Elie Wiesel spoke specifically about the risks of this very indifference and the importance of action. So few among the Germans acted, and certainly none acted early enough and decisively enough to change the fates of millions killed in the Holocaust. The past cannot be changed, but as Wiesel reminds the modern listener, we can take lessons from the past with us into the future, changing our fates and preventing a repeat of the horrors of World War II.

Practice Test 4

Rupert Brooke. Niagara Falls.

1   SAMUEL BUTLER has a lot to answer for. But for him, a modern traveler could spend his
2   time peacefully admiring the scenery instead of feeling himself bound to dog the simple and
3   grotesque of the world for the sake of their too-human comments. It is his fault if a
4   peasant's *naïveté* has come to outweigh the beauty of rivers, and the remarks of clergymen
5   are more than mountains. It is very restful to give up all effort at observing human nature
6   and drawing social and political deductions from trifles, and to let oneself relapse into wide-
7   mouthed worship of the wonders of nature. And this is very easy at Niagara. Niagara means
8   nothing. It is not leading anywhere. It does not result from anything. It throws no light on
9   the effects of Protection, nor on the Facility for Divorce in America, nor on Corruption in
10 Public Life, nor on Canadian character, nor even on the Navy Bill. It is merely a great deal of
11 water falling over some cliffs. But it is very remarkably that. The human race, apt as a child
12 to destroy what it admires, has done its best to surround the Falls with every distraction,
13 incongruity, and vulgarity. Hotels, powerhouses, bridges, trams, picture post-cards, sham
14 legends, stalls, booths, rifle-galleries, and side-shows frame them about. And there are
15 Touts. Niagara is the central home and breeding-place for all the touts of earth. There are
16 touts insinuating, and touts raucous, greasy touts, brazen touts, and upper-class, refined,
17 gentlemanly, take-you-by-the-arm touts; touts who intimidate and touts who wheedle;
18 professionals, amateurs, and *dilettanti*, male and female; touts who would photograph you
19 with your arm round a young lady against a faked background of the sublimest cataract,
20 touts who would bully you into cars, char-à-bancs, elevators, or tunnels, or deceive you into
21 a carriage and pair, touts who would sell you picture post-cards, moccasins, sham Indian
22 beadwork, blankets, tee-pees, and crockery, and touts, finally, who have no apparent object
23 in the world, but just purely, simply, merely, incessantly, indefatigably, and ineffugibly to
24 tout. And in the midst of all this, overwhelming it all, are the Falls. He who sees them
25 instantly forgets humanity. They are not very high, but they are overpowering. They are
26 divided by an island into two parts, the Canadian and the American.

27 Half a mile or so above the Falls, on either side, the water of the great stream begins to run
28 more swiftly and in confusion. It descends with ever-growing speed. It begins chattering and
29 leaping, breaking into a thousand ripples, throwing up joyful fingers of spray. Sometimes it
30 is divided by islands and rocks, sometimes the eye can see nothing but a waste of laughing,
31 springing, foamy waves, turning, crossing, even seeming to stand for an instant erect, but
32 always borne impetuously forward like a crowd of triumphant feasters. Sit close down by it,

209

33   and you see a fragment of the torrent against the sky, mottled, steely, and foaming, leaping
34   onward in far-flung criss-cross strands of water. Perpetually the eye is on the point of
35   descrying a pattern in this weaving, and perpetually it is cheated by change. In one place
36   part of the flood plunges over a ledge a few feet high and a quarter of a mile or so long, in a
37   uniform and stable curve. It gives an impression of almost military concerted movement,
38   grown suddenly out of confusion. But it is swiftly lost again in the multitudinous tossing
39   merriment. Here and there a rock close to the surface is marked by a white wave that faces
40   backwards and seems to be rushing madly up-stream, but is really stationary in the
41   headlong charge. But for these signs of reluctance, the waters seem to fling themselves on
42   with some foreknowledge of their fate, in an ever wilder frenzy. But it is no Maeterlinckian
43   prescience. They prove, rather, that Greek belief that the great crashes are preceded by a
44   louder merriment and a wilder gaiety. Leaping in the sunlight, careless, entwining,
45   clamorously joyful, the waves riot on towards the verge.

46   But there they change. As they turn to the sheer descent, the white and blue and slate
47   color, in the heart of the Canadian Falls at least, blend and deepen to a rich, wonderful,
48   luminous green. On the edge of disaster the river seems to gather herself, to pause, to lift a
49   head noble in ruin, and then, with a slow grandeur, to plunge into the eternal thunder and
50   white chaos below. Where the stream runs shallower it is a kind of violet color, but both
51   violet and green fray and frill to white as they fall. The mass of water, striking some ever-
52   hidden base of rock, leaps up the whole two hundred feet again in pinnacles and domes of
53   spray. The spray falls back into the lower river once more; all but a little that fines to foam
54   and white mist, which drifts in layers along the air, graining it, and wanders out on the wind
55   over the trees and gardens and houses, and so vanishes.

1. "It is not leading anywhere. It does not result from anything. It throws no light on the effects of Protection, nor on the Facility for Divorce in America, nor on Corruption in Public Life, nor on Canadian character, nor even on the Navy Bill. It is merely a great deal of water falling over some cliffs." The previous section of text is an example of:
    a. Isocolon
    b. Parallelism
    c. Coenotes
    d. Mesodiplosis

2. What does "touts" most nearly mean?
    a. Sales people
    b. Con men
    c. Tour guides
    d. Tourists

3. The following, "throwing up joyful fingers of spray" is an example of what rhetorical device?
    a. Metaphor
    b. Parallelism
    c. Abstract language
    d. Personification

4. Which of the following illustrates repetition?
    a. "Laughing, springing, foamy waves"
    b. "Violet and green fray and frill"
    c. "Little that fines to foam and white mist"
    d. "Waters seem to fling themselves"

5. This excerpt is largely:
    a. Expository
    b. Descriptive
    c. Narrative
    d. Persuasive
6. The main idea of this passage is:
    a. A visit to Niagara Falls will be quite expensive.
    b. The Falls are remarkably beautiful.
    c. Niagara Falls is quite dangerous.
    d. Everyone should visit Niagara Falls
7. What is the intended purpose of the figurative language in this passage?
    a. To entertain the reader
    b. To share the experience of Niagara Falls
    c. To describe a visit to the Falls
    d. To educate the reader about waterfalls
8. "But for these signs of reluctance, the waters seem to fling themselves on with some foreknowledge of their fate, in an ever wilder frenzy." This line is an example of:
    a. An analogy
    b. An anecdote
    c. An epithet
    d. A simile

9. "It is merely a great deal of water falling over some cliffs." This sentence is an example of:
    a. Figurative language
    b. Understatement
    c. Abstract language
    d. Metaphor
10. "Trifles" most closely means:
    a. Unimportant things
    b. Important things
    c. Nature
    d. Touts
11. "Not very high" is an example of:
    a. Figurative language
    b. Concrete language
    c. Parallelism
    d. Understatement

William McFee. The Market.

1   THERE is a sharp, imperative rap on my outer door; a rap having within its insistent urgency
2   a shadow of delicate diffidence, as though the person responsible were a trifle scared of the
3   performance and on tiptoe to run away. I roll over and regard the clock. Four-forty. One of
4   the dubious by-products of continuous service as a senior assistant at sea is the habit of
5   waking automatically about 4 A. M. This gives one several hours, when ashore, to meditate
6   upon one's sins, frailties, and (more rarely) triumphs and virtues. For a man who gets up at
7   say four-thirty is regarded with aversion ashore. His family express themselves with
8   superfluous vigor. He must lie still and meditate, or suffer the ignominy of being asked
9   when he is going away again.

10 But this morning, in these old Chambers in an ancient Inn buried in the heart of London City,
11 I have agreed to get up and go out. The reason for this momentous departure from a life of
12 temporary but deliberate indolence is a lady. "Cherchez la femme," as the French say with
13 the dry animosity of a logical race. Well, she is not far to seek, being on the outside of my
14 heavy oak door, tapping, as already hinted, with a sharp insistent delicacy. To this romantic
15 summons I reply with an articulate growl of acquiescence, and proceed to get ready. To
16 relieve the anxiety of any reader who imagines an impending elopement it may be stated in
17 succinct truthfulness that we are bound on no such desperate venture. We are going round
18 the corner a few blocks up the Strand, to Covent Garden Market, to see the arrival of the
19 metropolitan supply of produce.

20 Having accomplished a hasty toilet, almost as primitive as that favored by gentlemen
21 aroused to go on watch, and placating an occasional repetition of the tapping by brief
22 protests and reports of progress, I take hat and cane, and drawing the huge antique bolts of
23 my door, discover a young woman standing by the window looking out upon the quadrangle
24 of the old Inn. She is a very decided young woman, who is continually thinking out what she
25 calls "stunts" for articles in the press. That is her profession, or one of her professions—
26 writing articles for the press. The other profession is selling manuscripts, which constitutes
27 the tender bond between us. For the usual agent's commission she is selling one of my
28 manuscripts. Being an unattached and, as it were, unprotected male, she plans little
29 excursions about London to keep me instructed and entertained. Here she is attired in the
30 flamboyant finery of a London flowergirl. She is about to get the necessary copy for a
31 special article in a morning paper. With the exception of a certain expectant flash of her
32 bright black Irish eyes, she is entirely businesslike. Commenting on the beauty of an early
33 summer morning in town, we descend, and passing out under the ponderous ancient
34 archway, we make our leisurely progress westward down the Strand.

London is always beautiful to those who love and understand that extraordinary microcosm; but at five of a summer morning there is about her an exquisite quality of youthful fragrance and debonair freshness which goes to the heart. The newly-hosed streets are shining in the sunlight as though paved with "patines of bright gold." Early 'buses rumble by from neighboring barns where they have spent the night. And, as we near the new Gaiety Theatre, thrusting forward into the great rivers of traffic soon to pour round its base like some bold Byzantine promontory, we see Waterloo Bridge thronged with wagons, piled high. From all quarters they are coming, past Charing Cross the great wains are arriving from Paddington Terminal, from the market-garden section of Middlesex and Surrey. Down Wellington Street come carts laden with vegetables from Brentwood and Coggeshall, and neat vans packed with crates of watercress which grows in the lush lowlands of Suffolk and Cambridgeshire, and behind us are thundering huge four-horse vehicles from the docks, vehicles with peaches from South Africa, potatoes from the Canary Islands, onions from France, apples from California, oranges from the West Indies, pineapples from Central America, grapes from Spain and bananas from Colombia.

12. The phrase "delicate diffidence" is an example of:
    a. Metaphor
    b. Alliteration
    c. Repetition
    d. Parallelism

13. This passage is an example of a:
    a. Expository essay
    b. Narrative
    c. Argumentative essay
    d. Persuasive essay

14. "From all quarters they are coming, past Charing Cross the great wains are arriving from Paddington Terminal, from the market-garden section of Middlesex and Surrey. Down Wellington Street come carts laden with vegetables from Brentwood and Coggeshall, and neat vans packed with crates of watercress which grows in the lush lowlands of Suffolk and Cambridgeshire, and behind us are thundering huge four-horse vehicles from the docks, vehicles with peaches from South Africa, potatoes from the Canary Islands, onions from France, apples from California, oranges from the West Indies, pineapples from Central America, grapes from Spain and bananas from Colombia." This excerpt is an example of:
    a. A compound sentence
    b. An analogy
    c. A complex sentence
    d. A metaphor

15. These adjectives, "youthful fragrance and debonair freshness" suggest:
    a. Personification
    b. Allusion
    c. Anecdote
    d. Satire

16. The lady knocking on the door is:
    a. A flower girl
    b. The narrator's wife
    c. A reporter
    d. A noble lady

17. Where are they going?
    a. The Gaiety Theater
    b. The market
    c. Church
    d. The booksellers

18. In this usage, "decided" most likely means:
    a. Chose
    b. Insulted
    c. Determined
    d. Young

19. This piece is written in:
    a. Second person
    b. Third person
    c. Third person omniscient
    d. First person

20. "Being an unattached and, as it were, unprotected male, she plans little excursions about London to keep me instructed and entertained." What is unusual about this sentence?
    a. The subordinate clause begins the sentence.
    b. The typical gender roles are reversed.
    c. The trips are planned for the writer's benefit.
    d. The two have a professional relationship.

21. "Indolence" most likely means:
    a. Hard work
    b. Laziness
    c. Luxury
    d. Poverty

22. This essay is an example of:
    a. Prose
    b. Poetry
    c. Verse
    d. Drama

A.A. Milne. A Word for Autumn.

1   LAST night the waiter put the celery on with the cheese, and I knew that summer was
2   indeed dead. Other signs of autumn there may be—the reddening leaf, the chill in the early-
3   morning air, the misty evenings—but none of these comes home to me so truly. There may
4   be cool mornings in July; in a year of drought the leaves may change before their time; it is
5   only with the first celery that summer is over.

6   I knew all along that it would not last. Even in April I was saying that winter would soon be
7   here. Yet somehow it had begun to seem possible lately that a miracle might happen, that
8   summer might drift on and on through the months—a final upheaval to crown a wonderful
9   year. The celery settled that. Last night with the celery autumn came into its own.

10   There is a crispness about celery that is of the essence of October. It is as fresh and clean as
11   a rainy day after a spell of heat. It crackles pleasantly in the mouth. Moreover it is excellent,
12   I am told, for the complexion. One is always hearing of things which are good for the
13   complexion, but there is no doubt that celery stands high on the list. After the burns and
14   freckles of summer one is in need of something. How good that celery should be there at
15   one's elbow.

16   A week ago—("A little more cheese, waiter")—a week ago I grieved for the dying summer. I
17   wondered how I could possibly bear the waiting—the eight long months till May. In vain to
18   comfort myself with the thought that I could get through more work in the winter
19   undistracted by thoughts of cricket grounds and country houses. In vain, equally, to tell
20   myself that I could stay in bed later in the mornings. Even the thought of after-breakfast
21   pipes in front of the fire left me cold. But now, suddenly, I am reconciled to autumn. I see
22   quite clearly that all good things must come to an end. The summer has been splendid, but
23   it has lasted long enough. This morning I welcomed the chill in the air; this morning I viewed
24   the falling leaves with cheerfulness; and this morning I said to myself, "Why, of course, I'll
25   have celery for lunch." ("More bread, waiter.")

26   "Season of mists and mellow fruitfulness," said Keats, not actually picking out celery in so
27   many words, but plainly including it in the general blessings of the autumn. Yet what an
28   opportunity he missed by not concentrating on that precious root. Apples, grapes, nuts, and
29   vegetable marrows he mentions specially—and how poor a selection! For apples and grapes
30   are not typical of any month, so ubiquitous are they, vegetable marrows are
31   vegetables *pour rire* and have no place in any serious consideration of the seasons, while as
32   for nuts, have we not a national song which asserts distinctly, "Here we go gathering nuts in
33   May"? Season of mists and mellow celery, then let it be. A pat of butter underneath the
34   bough, a wedge of cheese, a loaf of bread and—Thou.

23. To what does "Thou" in the last line refer?
    a. Fall
    b. The narrator
    c. Cheese
    d. Celery

24. What is the mood of this piece?
    a. Melancholy
    b. Hopeful
    c. Frightening
    d. Dramatic

25. Celery is compared to:
    a. Cheese
    b. Butter
    c. Summer
    d. October

26. "Season of mists and mellow fruitfulness" refers to?
    a. Summer
    b. Autumn
    c. Spring
    d. Winter

27. What is the author's objection to Keats' quote?
    a. It relies upon false authority.
    b. It evokes an inaccurate impression of fall.
    c. It includes apples and grapes, but not celery.
    d. It shows a dislike for fall.

28. The following quote is an example of what, "have we not a national song which asserts distinctly, "Here we go gathering nuts in May"?
    a. A rhetorical question
    b. Figurative language
    c. A compound sentence
    d. A declarative sentence

29. "Pour rire" connotes what?
    a. These are important vegetables.
    b. These are rarely eaten.
    c. These are unimportant.
    d. These are not vegetables.

30. "A week ago—("A little more cheese, waiter")—a week ago I grieved for the dying summer. I wondered how I could possibly bear the waiting—the eight long months till May." This sentence contains which of the following:
    a. Abstract language
    b. A parenthetical phrase
    c. Alliteration
    d. An anecdote

31. "There is a crispness about celery that is of the essence of October. It is as fresh and clean as a rainy day after a spell of heat. It crackles pleasantly in the mouth. Moreover it is excellent, I am told, for the complexion. One is always hearing of things which are good for the complexion, but there is no doubt that celery stands high on the list. After the burns and freckles of summer one is in need of something. How good that celery should be there at one's elbow." This passage is figurative, but also:
    a. Allegorical
    b. Colloquial
    c. Formal
    d. Abstract

32. This essay includes all of the following elements:
    a. Narrative, figurative language
    b. Exposition, interrogatory sentences
    c. Allegory, figurative language
    d. Formal language, allegory

33. What time of year is it?
    a. October
    b. May
    c. April
    d. July

Philip Guedala. Some Historians.

IT was Quintillian or Mr. Max Beerbohm who said, "History repeats itself: historians repeat each other." The saying is full of the mellow wisdom of either writer, and stamped with the peculiar veracity of the Silver Age of Roman or British epigram. One might have added, if the aphorist had stayed for an answer, that history is rather interesting when it repeats itself: historians are not. In France, which is an enlightened country enjoying the benefits of the Revolution and a public examination in rhetoric, historians are expected to write in a single and classical style of French. The result is sometimes a rather irritating uniformity; it is one long Taine that has no turning, and any quotation may be attributed with safety to Guizot, because *la nuit tous les chats sont gris*. But in England, which is a free country, the restrictions natural to ignorant (and immoral) foreigners are put off by the rough island race, and history is written in a dialect which is not curable by education, and cannot (it would seem) be prevented by injunction.

Historians' English is not a style; it is an industrial disease. The thing is probably scheduled in the Workmen's Compensation Act, and the publisher may be required upon notice of the attack to make a suitable payment to the writer's dependants. The workers in this dangerous trade are required to adopt (like Mahomet's coffin) a detached standpoint—that is, to write as if they took no interest in the subject. Since it is not considered good form for a graduate of less than sixty years' standing to write upon any period that is either familiar or interesting, this feeling is easily acquired, and the resulting narrations present the dreary impartiality of the Recording Angel without that completeness which is the sole attraction of his style. Wilde complained of Mr. Hall Caine that he wrote at the top of his voice; but a modern historian, when he is really detached, writes like some one talking in the next room, and few writers have equaled the legal precision of Coxe's observation that the Turks "sawed the Archbishop and the Commandant in half, and committed other grave violations of international law."

Having purged his mind of all unsteadying interest in the subject, the young historian should adopt a moral code of more than Malthusian severity, which may be learned from any American writer of the last century upon the Renaissance or the decadence of Spain. This manner, which is especially necessary in passages dealing with character, will lend to his work the grave dignity that is requisite for translation into Latin prose, that supreme test of an historian's style. It will be his misfortune to meet upon the byways of history the oddest and most abnormal persons, and he should keep by him (unless he wishes to forfeit his Fellowship) some convenient formula by which he may indicate at once the enormity of the subject and the disapproval of the writer. The writings of Lord Macaulay will furnish him at need with the necessary facility in lightning characterization. It was the practice of Cicero to

36 label his contemporaries without distinction as "heavy men," and the characters of history
37 are easily divisible into "far-seeing statesmen" and "reckless libertines." It may be objected
38 that although it is sufficient for the purposes of contemporary caricature to represent Mr.
39 Gladstone as a collar or Mr. Chamberlain as an eye-glass, it is an inadequate record for
40 posterity. But it is impossible for a busy man to write history without formulæ, and after all
41 sheep are sheep and goats are goats. Lord Macaulay once wrote of some one, "In private
42 life he was stern, morose, and inexorable"; he was probably a Dutchman. It is a passage
43 which has served as a lasting model for the historian's treatment of character. I had always
44 imagined that Cliché was a suburb of Paris, until I discovered it to be a street in Oxford.
45 Thus, if the working historian is faced with a period of "deplorable excesses," he handles it
46 like a man, and writes always as if he was illustrated with steel engravings.

34. In line 3, "veracity" most closely means:
    a. Proof
    b. Truth
    c. Fidelity
    d. Conformity

35. "Aphorist" in line 4 most likely means:
    a. Writer
    b. Politician
    c. Speaker
    d. Intellectual

36. "But in England, which is a free country, the restrictions natural to ignorant (and immoral) foreigners are put off by the rough island race, and history is written in a dialect which is not curable by education, and cannot (it would seem) be prevented by injunction." The previous sentence illustrates:
    a. Figurative language
    b. Aphorisms
    c. Parenthetical phrases
    d. Expletives

37. Based on the information in the passage, the author is:
    a. British
    b. French
    c. German
    d. American

38. "Historians' English is not a style; it is an industrial disease." This is an example of:
    a. A metaphor
    b. A simile
    c. An expository fact
    d. A descriptive sentence

39. The thesis of this passage is:
    a. History is boring.
    b. Historians are boring.
    c. History is not important.
    d. History is very important.

40. The following, "sheep are sheep and goats are goats," is a :
    a. Cliché
    b. Epithet
    c. Eulogy
    d. Cacophony

41. "Malthusian severity" is a:
    a. Simile
    b. Metaphor
    c. Allusion
    d. Allegory

42. What factor is responsible for the quality of historical writing:
    a. The historical period
    b. Education
    c. Government
    d. Impartiality

43. What is "that supreme test of an historian's style" referred to in lines 30-31?
    a. Impartiality
    b. Formulaic writing
    c. Translation into Latin
    d. Disapproval

44. This essay begins with:
    a. An emotional appeal
    b. An epigraph
    c. An expletive
    d. An interjection

1 THE rain flashed across the midnight window with a myriad feet. There was a groan in outer
2 darkness, the voice of all nameless dreads. The nervous candle-flame shuddered by my
3 bedside. The groaning rose to a shriek, and the little flame jumped in a panic, and nearly left
4 its white column. Out of the corners of the room swarmed the released shadows. Black
5 specters danced in ecstasy over my bed. I love fresh air, but I cannot allow it to slay the
6 shining and delicate body of my little friend the candle-flame, the comrade who ventures
7 with me into the solitudes beyond midnight. I shut the window.

8 They talk of the candle-power of an electric bulb. What do they mean? It cannot have the
9 faintest glimmer of the real power of my candle. It would be as right to express, in the same
10 inverted and foolish comparison, the worth of "those delicate sisters, the Pleiades." That
11 pinch of star dust, the Pleiades, exquisitely remote in deepest night, in the profound where
12 light all but fails, has not the power of a sulphur match; yet, still apprehensive to the mind
13 though tremulous on the limit of vision, and sometimes even vanishing, it brings into
14 distinction those distant and difficult hints—hidden far behind all our verified thoughts—
15 which we rarely properly view. I should like to know of any great arc-lamp which could do
16 that. So the star-like candle for me. No other light follows so intimately an author's most
17 ghostly suggestion. We sit, the candle and I, in the midst of the shades we are conquering,
18 and sometimes look up from the lucent page to contemplate the dark hosts of the enemy
19 with a smile before they overwhelm us; as they will, of course. Like me, the candle is mortal;
20 it will burn out.

21 As the bed-book itself should be a sort of night-light, to assist its illumination, coarse lamps
22 are useless. They would douse the book. The light for such a book must accord with it. It
23 must be, like the book, a limited, personal, mellow, and companionable glow; the solitary
24 taper beside the only worshiper in a sanctuary. That is why nothing can compare with the
25 intimacy of candle-light for a bed-book. It is a living heart, bright and warm in central night,
26 burning for us alone, holding the gaunt and towering shadows at bay. There the monstrous
27 specters stand in our midnight room, the advance guard of the darkness of the world, held
28 off by our valiant little glim, but ready to flood instantly and founder us in original gloom.

29   The wind moans without; ancient evils are at large and wandering in torment. The rain
30 shrieks across the window. For a moment, for just a moment, the sentinel candle is shaken,
31 and burns blue with terror. The shadows leap out instantly. The little flame recovers, and
32 merely looks at its foe the darkness, and back to its own place goes the old enemy of light
33 and man. The candle for me, tiny, mortal, warm, and brave, a golden lily on a silver stem!

34 "Almost any book does for a bed-book," a woman once said to me. I nearly replied in a
35 hurry that almost any woman would do for a wife; but that is not the way to bring people to
36 conviction of sin. Her idea was that the bed-book is soporific, and for that reason she even
37 advocated the reading of political speeches. That would be a dissolute act. Certainly you
38 would go to sleep; but in what a frame of mind! You would enter into sleep with your eyes
39 shut. It would be like dying, not only unshriven, but in the act of guilt.

45. To what does, "the old enemy of light and man" in line 32 refer?
    a. The candle
    b. The bed-book
    c. Darkness
    d. Shadows

46. "Soporific" in line 36 most likely means:
    a. Sleep-inducing
    b. Boring
    c. Dark
    d. Depressing

47. The following, "a limited, personal, mellow, and companionable glow" is an example of:
    a. An aphorism
    b. A metaphor
    c. Abstract language
    d. Descriptive language

48. Throughout this passage, the author uses:
    a. Colloquialisms
    b. Clichés
    c. Simple sentences
    d. Figurative language

49. The use of language in this piece may be described as:
    a. Formal
    b. Expository
    c. Poetic
    d. Descriptive

50. Comparing the candle to starlight is an example of:
    a. Understatement
    b. Hyperbole
    c. An aphorism
    d. Parallelism

51. Which of the following illustrates personification?
    a. "The little flame recovers, and merely looks at its foe the darkness"
    b. "Has not the power of a sulphur match"
    c. "The bed-book is soporific"
    d. "As the bed-book itself should be a sort of night-light"

52. In the following, what is the sin, " I nearly replied in a hurry that almost any woman would do for a wife; but that is not the way to bring people to conviction of sin."
    a. The use of electric lights
    b. Blowing out the candle
    c. Reading any book as a bed-book
    d. Not reading in bed

53. What is the antecedent for it in this sentence in line 41 and 42, "It would be like dying, not only unshriven, but in the act of guilt."
    a. Reading political speeches before bed
    b. Reading before bed
    c. Taking any woman as a wife
    d. Dying while you read

54. The author is:
    a. Narrating his experiences reading in bed
    b. Explaining why you should read in bed
    c. Arguing for the value of candles while reading in bed
    d. Explaining how candles can be used

55. "The wind moans without; ancient evils are at large and wandering in torment. The rain shrieks across the window." Words like "moans" and "shrieks" in this sentence show the use of:
   a. Imagery
   b. Aphorisms
   c. Parallelism
   d. Onomatopoeia

From Edgar Allen Poe's The Philosophy of Composition. Read this passage and write an essay explaining how Poe used language and rhetoric in his writing.

There is a radical error, I think, in the usual mode of constructing a story. Either history affords a thesis—or one is suggested by an incident of the day—or, at best, the author sets himself to work in the combination of striking events to form merely the basis of his narrative—designing, generally, to fill in with description, dialogue, or autorial comment, whatever crevices of fact, or action, may, from page to page, render themselves apparent.

I prefer commencing with the consideration of an effect. Keeping originality *always* in view—for he is false to himself who ventures to dispense with so obvious and so easily attainable a source of interest—I say to myself, in the first place, "Of the innumerable effects, or impressions, of which the heart, the intellect, or (more generally) the soul is susceptible, what one shall I, on the present occasion, select?" Having chosen a novel, first, and secondly a vivid effect, I consider whether it can be best wrought by incident or tone—whether by ordinary incidents and peculiar tone, or the converse, or by peculiarity both of incident and tone—afterward looking about me (or rather within) for such combinations of event, or tone, as shall best aid me in the construction of the effect.

I have often thought how interesting a magazine paper might be written by any author who would—that is to say, who could—detail, step by step, the processes by which any one of his compositions attained its ultimate point of completion. Why such a paper has never been given to the world, I am much at a loss to say—but, perhaps, the autorial vanity has had more to do with the omission than any one other cause. Most writers—poets in especial—prefer having it understood that they compose by a species of fine frenzy—an ecstatic intuition—and would positively shudder at letting the public take a peep behind the scenes, at the elaborate and vacillating crudities of thought—at the true purposes seized only at the last moment—at the innumerable glimpses of idea that arrived not at the maturity of full view—at the fully matured fancies discarded in despair as unmanageable— at the cautious selections and rejections—at the painful erasures and interpolations—in a word, at the wheels and pinions—the tackle for scene-shifting—the step-ladders and demon-traps—the cock's feathers, the red paint and the black patches, which, in ninety-nine cases out of the hundred, constitute the properties of the literary *histrio*.

I am aware, on the other hand, that the case is by no means common, in which an author is at all in condition to retrace the steps by which his conclusions have been attained. In general, suggestions, having arisen pell-mell, are pursued and forgotten in a similar manner.

For my own part, I have neither sympathy with the repugnance alluded to, nor, at any time, the least difficulty in recalling to mind the progressive steps of any of my compositions; and, since the interest of an analysis, or reconstruction, such as I have considered a *desideratum*, is quite independent of any real or fancied interest in the thing analyzed, it will not be regarded as a breach of decorum on my part to show the *modus operandi* by which some one of my own works was put together. I select "The Raven," as the most generally known. It is my design to render it manifest that no one point in its composition is referable either to accident or intuition—that the work proceeded, step by step, to its completion with the precision and rigid consequence of a mathematical problem.

This short excerpt, taken from Nicholas Murray Butler's The Revolt of the Unfit discusses the understanding of evolution. Your argumentative essay should refute, support or qualify this text and its impression of evolution.

THERE are wars and rumors of wars in a portion of the territory occupied by the doctrine of organic evolution. All is not working smoothly and well and according to formula. It begins to appear that those men of science who, having derived the doctrine of organic evolution in its modern form from observations on earthworms, on climbing-plants, and on brightly colored birds, and who then straightway applied it blithely to man and his affairs, have made enemies of no small part of the human race.

It was all well enough to treat some earthworms, some climbing-plants, and some brightly colored birds as fit, and others as unfit, to survive; but when this distinction is extended over human beings and their economic, social, and political affairs, there is a general pricking-up of ears. The consciously fit look down on the resulting discussions with complacent scorn. The consciously unfit rage and roar loudly; while the unconsciously unfit bestir themselves mightily to overturn the whole theory upon which the distinction between fitness and unfitness rests. If any law of nature makes so absurd a distinction as that, then the offending and obnoxious law must be repealed, and that quickly.

The trouble appears to arise primarily from the fact that man does not like what may be termed his evolutionary poor relations. He is willing enough to read about earthworms and climbing-plants and brightly colored birds, but he does not want nature to be making leaps from any of these to him.

The earthworm, which, not being adapted to its surroundings, soon dies unhonored and unsung, passes peacefully out of life without either a coroner's inquest, an indictment for earthworm slaughter, a legislative proposal for the future protection of earthworms, or even a new society for the reform of the social and economic state of the earthworms that are left. Even the quasi-intelligent climbing-plant and the brightly colored bird, humanly vain, find an equally inconspicuous fate awaiting them. This is the way nature operates when unimpeded or unchallenged by the powerful manifestations of human revolt or human revenge. Of course if man understood the place assigned to him in nature by the doctrine of organic evolution as well as the earthworm, the climbing-plant, and the brightly colored bird understand theirs, he, too, like them, would submit to nature's processes and decrees without a protest. As a matter of logic, no doubt he ought to; but after all these centuries, it is still a far cry from logic to life.

In fact, man, unless he is consciously and admittedly fit, revolts against the implication of the doctrine of evolution, and objects both to being considered unfit to survive and succeed, and to being forced to accept the only fate which nature offers to those who are unfit for survival and success. Indeed, he manifests with amazing pertinacity what Schopenhauer used to call "the will to live," and considerations and arguments based on adaptability to environment have no weight with him. So much the worse for environment, he cries; and straightway sets out to prove it.

On the other hand, those humans who are classed by the doctrine of evolution as fit, exhibit a most disconcerting satisfaction with things as they are. The fit make no conscious struggle for existence. They do not have to. Being fit, they survive *ipso facto*. Thus does the doctrine of evolution, like a playful kitten, merrily pursue its tail with rapturous delight. The fit survive; those survive who are fit. Nothing could be more simple.

These excerpts all deal with the impact of the changing understanding of the world, including geology and evolution. Synthesize at least two to three of these works into a single analysis.

H.G. Wells. The Discovery of the Future.

But modern science, that is to say the relentless systematic criticism of phenomena, has in the past hundred years absolutely destroyed the conception of a finitely distant beginning of things; has abolished such limits to the past as a dated creation set, and added an enormous vista to that limited sixteenth century outlook. And what I would insist upon is that this further knowledge is a new kind of knowledge, obtained in a new kind of way. We know to-day, quite as confidently and in many respects more intimately than we know Sargon or Zenobia or Caractacus, the form and the habits of creatures that no living being has ever met, that no human eye has ever regarded, and the character of scenery that no man has ever seen or can ever possibly see; we picture to ourselves the labyrinthodon raising its clumsy head above the water of the carboniferous swamps in which he lived, and we figure the pterodactyls, those great bird lizards, flapping their way athwart the forests of the Mesozoic age with exactly the same certainty as that with which we picture the rhinoceros or the vulture. I doubt no more about the facts in this farther picture than I do about those in the nearest. I believe in the megatherium which I have never seen as confidently as I believe in the hippopotamus that has engulfed buns from my hand. A vast amount of detail in that farther picture is now fixed and finite for all time. And a countless number of investigators are persistently and confidently enlarging, amplifying, correcting, and pushing farther and farther back the boundaries of this greater past—this prehuman past—that the scientific criticism of existing phenomena has discovered and restored and brought for the first time into the world of human thought. We have become possessed of a new and once unsuspected history of the world—of which all the history that was known, for example, to Dr. Johnson is only the brief concluding chapter; and even that concluding chapter has been greatly enlarged and corrected by the exploring archæologists working strictly upon the lines of the new method—that is to say, the comparison and criticism of suggestive facts.

I want particularly to insist upon this, that all this outer past—this non-historical past—is the product of a new and keener habit of inquiry, and no sort of revelation. It is simply due to a new and more critical way of looking at things. Our knowledge of the geological past, clear and definite as it has become, is of a different and lower order than the knowledge of our memory, and yet of a quite practicable and trustworthy order—a knowledge good enough to go upon; and if one were to speak of the private memory as the personal past, of the next wider area of knowledge as the traditional or historical past, then one might call all that great and inspiring background[31] of remoter geological time the inductive past.

And this great discovery of the inductive past was got by the discussion and rediscussion and effective criticism of a number of existing facts, odd-shaped lumps of stone, streaks and bandings in quarries and cliffs, anatomical and developmental detail that had always been about in the world, that had been lying at the feet of mankind so long as mankind had existed, but that no one had ever dreamed before could supply any information at all, much more reveal such astounding and enlightening vistas. Looked at in a new way they became sources of dazzling and penetrating light. The remoter past lit up and became a picture. Considered as effects, compared and criticised, they yielded a clairvoyant vision of the history of interminable years.

And now, if it has been possible for men by picking out a number of suggestive and significant looking things in the present, by comparing them, criticising them, and discussing them, with a perpetual insistence upon "Why?" without any guiding tradition, and indeed in the teeth of established beliefs, to construct this amazing searchlight of inference into the remoter past, is it really, after all, such an extravagant and hopeless thing to suggest that, by seeking for operating causes instead of for fossils, and by criticising them as persistently and thoroughly as the geological record has been criticised, it may be possible to throw a searchlight of inference forward instead of backward, and to attain to a knowledge of coming things as clear, as universally convincing, and infinitely more important to mankind than the clear vision of the past that geology has opened to us during the nineteenth century?

"Wealden!" cried Challenger, in an ecstasy. "I've seen them in the Wealden clay. It is a creature walking erect upon three-toed feet, and occasionally putting one of its five-fingered forepaws upon the ground. Not a bird, my dear Roxton—not a bird."

"A beast?"

"No; a reptile—a dinosaur. Nothing else could have left such a track. They puzzled a worthy Sussex doctor some ninety years ago; but who in the world could have hoped—hoped—to have seen a sight like that?"

His words died away into a whisper, and we all stood in motionless amazement. Following the tracks, we had left the morass and passed through a screen of brushwood and trees. Beyond was an open glade, and in this were five of the most extraordinary creatures that I have ever seen. Crouching down among the bushes, we observed them at our leisure.

There were, as I say, five of them, two being adults and three young ones. In size they were enormous. Even the babies were as big as elephants, while the two large ones were far beyond all creatures I have ever seen. They had slate-colored skin, which was scaled like a lizard's and shimmered where the sun shone upon it. All five were sitting up, balancing themselves upon their broad, powerful tails and their huge three-toed hind-feet, while with their small five-fingered front-feet they pulled down the branches upon which they browsed. I do not know that I can bring their appearance home to you better than by saying that they looked like monstrous kangaroos, twenty feet in length, and with skins like black crocodiles.

I do not know how long we stayed motionless gazing at this marvelous spectacle. A strong wind blew towards us and we were well concealed, so there was no chance of discovery. From time to time the little ones played round their parents in unwieldy gambols, the great beasts bounding into the air and falling with dull thuds upon the earth. The strength of the parents seemed to be limitless, for one of them, having some difficulty in reaching a bunch of foliage which grew upon a considerable-sized tree, put his fore-legs round the trunk and tore it down as if it had been a sapling. The action seemed, as I thought, to show not only the great development of its muscles, but also the small one of its brain, for the whole weight came crashing down upon the top of it, and it uttered a series of shrill yelps to show that, big as it was, there was a limit to what it could endure. The incident made it think, apparently, that the neighborhood was dangerous, for it slowly lurched off through the wood, followed by its mate and its three enormous infants. We saw the shimmering slaty gleam of their skins between the tree-trunks, and their heads undulating high above the brush-wood. Then they vanished from our sight.

William Diller Matthew. Dinosaurs.

"As now exhibited in the Dinosaur Hall, this group gives to the imaginative observer a most vivid picture of a characteristic scene in that bygone age, millions of years ago, when reptiles were the lords of creation, and 'Nature, red in tooth and claw' had lost none of her primitive savagery, and the era of brute force and ferocity showed little sign of the gradual amelioration which was to come to pass in future ages through the predominance of superior intelligence."

Appearance and Habits of Allosaurus. A study of the mechanism of the Allosaurus skeleton shows us in the first place that the animal is balanced on the hind [43] limbs, the long heavy tail making an adequate counterpoise for the short compact body and head. The hind limbs are nine feet in length when extended, about equal to the length of the body and neck, and the bones are massively proportioned. When the thigh bone is set in its normal position, as indicated by the position of the scars and processes for attachment of the principal muscles (see under Brontosaurus for the method used to determine this), the knee bends forward as in mammals and birds, not outward as in most modern reptiles. The articulations of the foot bones show that the animal rested upon the ends of the metapodials, as birds and many mammals do, not upon the sole of the foot like crocodiles or lizards. The flat vertebral joints show that the short compact body was not as flexible as the longer body of crocodiles or lizards, in which the articulations are of the ball and socket type showing that in them this region was very flexible. The tail also shows a limited flexibility. It could not be curled or thrown over the back, but projected out behind the animal, swinging from side to side or up and down as much as was needed for balance. The curvature of the ribs shows that the body was narrow and deep, unlike the broad flattened body of the crocodile or the less flattened but still broad body of the lizard. The loose hung jaw, articulated far back, shows by the set of its muscles that it was capable of an enormous gape; while in the skull there is evidence of a limited movement of the upper jaw on the cranial portion, intended [44] probably to assist in the swallowing of large objects, like the double jointed jaw of a snake.

As to the nature of the skin we have no exact knowledge. We may be sure that it had no bony armor like the crocodile, for remains of any such armor could not fail to be preserved with the skeletons, as it always is in fossil crocodiles or turtles. Perhaps it was scaly like the skin of lizards and snakes, for the horny scales of the body are not preserved in fossil skeletons of these reptiles. But if so we might expect from the analogy of the lizard that the scales of the head would be ossified and preserved in the fossil; and there is nothing of this kind in the Carnivorous Dinosaurs. We can exclude feathers from consideration, for these dinosaurs have no affinities to birds, and there is no evidence for feathers in any dinosaur. Probably the best evidence is that of the Trachodon or duck-billed dinosaur although this animal was but distantly related to the Allosaurus. In Trachodon (see p. 94), we know that the skin bore neither feathers nor overlapping scales but had a curiously patterned mosaic of tiny polygonal plates and was thin and quite flexible. Some such type of skin as this, in default of better evidence, we may ascribe to the Allosaurus.

The natural belief on this subject doubtless is, that the world, such as we now see it, possessed its present form and configuration from the beginning. Nothing can be more natural than the belief that the present continents and oceans have always been where they are now; that we have always had the same mountains and plains; that our rivers have always had their present courses, and our lakes their present positions; that our climate has always been the same; and that our animals and plants have always been identical with those now familiar to us. Nothing could be more natural than such a belief, and nothing could be further removed from the actual truth. On the contrary, a very slight acquaintance with geology shows us, in the words of Sir John Herschel, that Page 7 "the actual configuration of our continents and islands, the coast-lines of our maps, the direction and elevation of our mountain-chains, the courses of our rivers, and the soundings of our oceans, are not things primordially arranged in the construction of our globe, but results of successive and complex actions on a former state of things; *that*, again, of similar actions on another still more remote; and so on, till the original and really permanent state is pushed altogether out of sight and beyond the reach even of imagination; while on the other hand, a similar, and, as far as we can see, interminable vista is opened out for the future, by which the habitability of our planet is secured amid the total abolition on it of the present theatres of terrestrial life."

Geology, then, teaches us that the physical features which now distinguish the earth's surface have been produced as the ultimate result of an almost endless succession of precedent changes. Palæontology teaches us, though not yet in such assured accents, the same lesson. Our present animals and plants have not been produced, in their innumerable forms, each as we now know it, as the sudden, collective, and simultaneous birth of a renovated world. On the contrary, we have the clearest evidence that some of our existing animals and plants made their appearance upon the earth at a much earlier period than others. In the confederation of animated nature some races can boast of an immemorial antiquity, whilst others are comparative *parvenus*. We have also the clearest evidence that the animals and plants which now inhabit the globe have been preceded, over and over again, by other different assemblages of animals and plants, which have flourished in successive periods of the earth's history, have reached their culmination, and then have given way to a fresh series of living beings. We have, finally, the clearest evidence that these successive groups of animals and plants (faunæ and floræ) are to a greater or less extent directly connected with one another. Each group is, to a greater or less extent, the lineal descendant of the group which immediately preceded it in point of time, and is more or less fully concerned with giving origin to the group which immediately follows it. That this law of "evolution" has prevailed to a great extent is quite certain; but it does not meet all the exigencies of the case, and it is probable that its action has been supplemented by some still unknown law of a different character.

We shall have to consider the question of geological "continuity" again. In the meanwhile, it is sufficient to state that this doctrine is now almost universally accepted as the basis of all inquiries, both in the domain of geology and that of palæontology. The advocates of continuity possess one immense advantage over those who believe in violent and revolutionary convulsions, that they call into play only agencies of which we have actual knowledge. We *know* that certain forces are now at work, producing certain modifications in the present condition of the globe; and we *know* that these forces are capable of producing the vastest of the changes which geology brings under our consideration, provided we assign a time proportionately vast for their operation. On the other hand, the advocates of catastrophism, to make good their views, are compelled to invoke forces and actions, both destructive and restorative, of which we have, and can have, no direct knowledge. They endow the whirlwind and the earthquake, the central fire and the rain from heaven, with powers as mighty as ever imagined in fable, and they build up the fragments of a repeatedly shattered world by the intervention of an intermittently active creative power.

Practice Test 4 Answer Key

1. d	2. a	3. d	4. a	5. b	6. b	7. b
8. a	9. b	10. a	11. d	12. b	13. b	14. a
15. a	16. c	17. b	18. c	19. d	20. b	21. b
22. a	23. d	24. b	25. d	26. b	27. c	28. a
29. c	30. b	31. b	32. a	33. a	34. b	35. d
36. c	37. a	38. a	39. b	40. a	41. c	42. d
43. c	44. b	45. c	46. a	47. d	48. d	49. c
50. b	51. a	52. c	53. a	54. c	55. a	

Expository Essay 4

Edgar Allen Poe, noted author, is writing about the art and craft of writing in The Philosophy of Composition. Poe writes in the first person, relying upon his own reputation to justify his argument and present his position on how one should write. Poe invites us into his essay with musings on the process of writing, but also sets the reader up for a look into his own creative process. His exposition on the subject of writing is highly personal, but as is suited to the author, relies upon figurative language. The reader can imagine the experience of the author, composing a work, even without understanding how the composition occurred. The tone of the essay transitions, as the content does. Poe's ability to create a mental image moves us from chaotic creation to calm.

For Poe, the effect of the work is first and foremost. This factor is more important than the theme, content or details. Effect, according to Poe, requires either incident or tone, or a combination of the two. This emphasis is echoed in his own essay, even if it is not a work of either fiction or poetry. While incident does not play a role in this philosophical essay about the process of writing, tone does. Poe interjects and interrupts himself, providing a glimpse into the fevered process of writing. His essay reads a bit like a journal, with additional notes and thoughts added as they come to him. The tone is hurried, rushed and inspired, frenzied to create, but still clear and coherent. His tone is created through the use of both syntax, as in his interrupted sentences with interjections and parenthetical phrases, as well as through the use of figurative language.

Poe's figurative language serves to create a mental image of the frenzy and rush of creation that many poets claim to experience. The author's experience is described as a process of picking out, selection and rejection. While this is first described clearly, Poe goes on to offer up a variety of figurative metaphors for the experience. These include "step-ladders and demon traps" and "wheels and pinions". These metaphors provide a visual reference for the experience of writing, one that might be otherwise inaccessible to the reader.

Distinguishing himself from his peers, Poe suggests that he, himself, is well aware of his own compositional process, with its leaps forward and steps backward. He describes this process as mathematical and logical. Here, his writing mimics the content. There is no more rushed fervor here. The syntax is clear, with a clean progression of thought and information. His creative process is not "pell-mell", but progressive.

While only a portion of Poe's The Philosophy of Composition is presented here, the text clearly illustrates the remarkable rhetorical skill. Poe inspires, through his words and syntax, an effect. We experience the poet's feelings during creation, contrasted with Poe's own. He offers us a look at the process of composition removed from this sort of chaos, defining it as a mathematical one. Here, poetry and composition have moved from the purely emotional to the logical.

Argumentative Essay 4

Butler's essay on The Revolt of the Unfit is focused not on the science of evolution, but the reaction to the still-new theory of evolution. Butler makes the argument that those that oppose the theory of evolution, here implying Darwin's survival of the fittest, themselves fear being unfit. They do not fear the notion of the survival of the fittest as applied to lower creatures, but when applied to the social and political realms of human society, it becomes, according to Butler, more problematic. Butler's essay moves from the realm of scientific evolution into the realm of social Darwinism, a much darker part of our evolutionary and social history.

First, we must understand the connotation of fit and unfit, for Butler. Fit, in this instance, specifically implies those who thrive. The fittest are those who succeed socially, politically and economically. They are the rich and powerful, or even the not-so-rich and not-so-powerful, but still comfortable. These individuals accept and support the status quo, because it benefits them. The unfit are the poor, the unsuccessful, the lower classes. Here, they do not like the status quo, instead seeking change. The change they seek, according to Butler, reduces competition. The implication is clear—this change is a socialist one.

Today, social science clearly disagrees with notions of the survival of the fittest as applied to societies. These theories led to practices of eugenics and even supported the ideologies of the Nazi party. Instead of assuming the survival of the fittest, we assess what can be done to improve the survival of all. Improved access to education, better resources, these things are used in the hope of bringing the unfit up to the level of the fit.

Even as social science has moved away from social evolution, there remain hints of this very theory within our society. The fit, the wealthy, think themselves better than the masses. Social liberalism is criticized as helping those too weak to help themselves. In some cases, the impact of social Darwinism remains present in our society. While these notions may be less violent than they were in the 1930s, they remain fundamentally similar. Some people are lesser than others, worth less and valued less.

Evolution is a physical, scientific theory. This theory, in its earliest form, stated that genetic adaptation was the result of the survival of the fittest. Survival in this case referred to genetic survival. Success was defined as living long enough to breed, rear young and pass along genes. This theory does not, in any fundamental way, relate to social organization. Even by the most basic definition of the survival of the fittest, the ability to survive and breed, whether one is fit or unfit is unrelated to social success. The "unfit" revolt not because they are unfit, but because of their social standing and social hierarchies. Butler's essay is a product of its time, suggestive of unfortunate movements that would forever mark the history of the 20th century.

245

Synthesis Essay 4

The 19th century brought about significant cultural change as the result of a changing understanding of science, geology and the world. This alteration in perspective was as significant as the realization that the earth was round and orbited the sun. Scientists were not the only ones to find that this had changed their world. These changes moved throughout society at all levels, from the highest to the lowest. Access to new resources in natural history allowed everyone to learn about geology, paleontology and other new sciences.

Books on geology and paleontology weren't just read by scientists. The public bought and read these books, as well as books on evolution. Many editions were designed for the general reader, like Dinosaurs. These books were written to be read by people with limited scientific knowledge. The grammar and syntax are simple, and the language relies upon clear concrete terminology. The authors willingly embrace figurative language when it will help the reader to make analogies to familiar creatures.

For the first time, a past before the time of written history or human creation was becoming available to the curious. Even today, dinosaurs and the most ancient past remain a fascination for many. The books of the 19th and early 20th century have been replaced by computer-generated documentaries and films. People flocked to museums to see newly-assembled skeletons and read about the lives of paleontologists looking for the most important new finds. These materials were written in response to that. They were the reality television of their day.

While these were not sciences that changed daily life, they found their way into both essays and fiction. H.G. Wells' Discovery of the Future directly addresses these new findings, and the impact of them. Here, Wells deals specifically with one of the most critical of these findings. The earth was no longer finite, defined by a short life span. With this realization, the possibilities of the sciences, from paleontology to astronomy increased remarkably. Now, there was the option for a "new kind of knowledge". As is appropriate for a text tackling science, Wells relies upon specific, concrete examples to add authority to his argument. Wells used concrete examples, while Arthur Conan Doyle took advantage of the new science to create a fictional novel, offering the reader the possibility to, himself, step back in time to walk with these exotic beasts. In this, Doyle integrated these discoveries into an adventure, but also made the scientists exploring this ancient world the heroes of his story.

Ideology and understanding changed in the 19th century. For the first time, humans became aware of all that had come before them and began to recognize their place in the history of the earth. Rather than being the center of creation, humanity was a relative latecomer to the world, following after the giants of the past.